D0210144

BEST OF

London

Sarah Johnstone

Best of London
3rd edition – September 2004
First published – April 2000

Published by Lonely Planet Publications Pty Ltd
ABN 36 005 607 983

Australia	Head Office, Locked Bag 1, Footscray, Vic 3011
	☎ 03 8379 8000 fax 03 8379 8111
	🖳 talk2us@lonelyplanet.com.au
USA	150 Linden St, Oakland, CA 94607
	☎ 510 893 8555 toll free 800 275 8555
	fax 510 893 8572
	🖳 info@lonelyplanet.com
UK	72–82 Rosebery Avenue, London EC1R 4RW
	☎ 020 7841 9000 fax 020 7841 9001
	🖳 go@lonelyplanet.co.uk

This title was commissioned in Lonely Planet's London office
and produced by: **Commissioning Editors** Alan Murphy
& Fiona Christie **Coordinating Editor** Adrienne Costanzo
Coordinating Cartographer Jolyon Philcox **Layout Designer**
David Kemp **Proofer** Nina Rousseau **Cartographers** GIS
Unit, Kim McDonald **Managing Cartographer** Mark Griffiths
Cover Designer Annika Roojun **Project Managers** Andrew
Weatherill & Charles Rawlings-Way **Series Designer** Gerilyn
Attebery **Mapping Development** Paul Piaia **Regional
Publishing Manager** Amanda Canning **Thanks to** Adriana
Mammarella, Fiona Siseman, Stephanie Pearson, Melanie
Dankel, Piotr Czajkowski

© Lonely Planet Publications Pty Ltd 2004.
All rights reserved.

Photographs by Lonely Planet Images and Neil Setchfield
except for the following: p64, p65, p66, p68, p70, p71,
p72, p74, p76, p77, p83, p86, p89, p98, p99, p101, p102
Jonathan Smith; p5 Martin Moos; p16, p26, p27 Charlotte
Hindle; p23 Manfred Gottschalk; p33, p90 Simon Bracken;
p42, p47 David Tomlinson; p44 Richard I'Anson; p46 Bryn
Thomas; p48 Guy Moberly; p50 Chris Mellor.
Cover photograph Tower Bridge, Manfred Gottschalk/
Lonely Planet Images. All images are copyright of the
photographers unless otherwise indicated. Many of the
images in this guide are available for licensing from
Lonely Planet Images: 🖳 www.lonelyplanetimages.com.

ISBN 1 74059 477 0

Printed through Colorcraft Ltd, Hong Kong
Printed in China

Acknowledgements London Underground Map: London
Transport Museum © 2004

Lonely Planet and the Lonely Planet logo are trademarks
of Lonely Planet and are registered in the US Patent and
Trademark Office and in other countries.

Lonely Planet does not allow its name or logo to be
appropriated by commercial establishments, such as
retailers, restaurants or hotels. Please let us know of any
misuses: 🖳 www.lonelyplanet.com/ip

HOW TO USE THIS BOOK

Colour-Coding & Maps

Each chapter has a colour code along the
banner at the top of the page which is also
used for text and symbols on maps (eg, all
venues reviewed in the Highlights chapter are
orange on the maps). The fold-out maps inside
the front and back covers are numbered from
1 to 6. All sights and venues in the text have
map references, eg (3, A4) means Map 3, grid
reference A4. See p128 for map symbols.

Prices

Multiple prices listed with reviews (eg £10/5)
usually indicate adult/concession admission to
a venue. Concession prices can include senior,
student, member or coupon discounts. Meal
cost and room-rate categories are listed at
the start of the Eating and Sleeping chapters,
respectively.

Text Symbols

☎	telephone
🖳	email/website address
✉	address
£	admission, costs
🕑	opening hours
ⓘ	information
🚌	bus
⚓	ferry
🚆	train/DLR
⊖	Underground
♿	wheelchair access
✗	on-site/nearby eatery
👶	child-friendly venue
V	good vegetarian selection

**Although the authors and Lonely Planet have taken all reasonable care in preparing this
book, we make no warranty about the accuracy or completeness of its content and, to the
maximum extent permitted, disclaim all liability arising from its use.**

Contents

From the Publisher

AUTHOR

Sarah Johnstone

Australian journalist Sarah Johnstone came to London planning to stay for a year, and more than 13 years later she's still here. Having worked for Reuters, *Business Traveller* and a range of other magazines, and as a poverty-stricken student while getting her MSc at the London School of Economics, she's seen the English capital from many sides. Working on this book and Lonely Planet's *London* city guide reopened her eyes to this vibrant city's fantastic cultural attractions – high and low. As she explored the city and ate in much better restaurants than she ever dared to expect, she realised how much London has improved in the past few years. Now, if only something could be done about the tube...

Thanks to all who accompanied me on my strange exploration of a place I thought I already knew, particularly Max, Inkeri, Richard and Jazmin. Thanks also to all the unknown people in press and box offices who answered my queries. Fiona Christie at Lonely Planet was kind enough to give me the gig, and Adrienne Costanzo and Charles Rawlings-Way kept it on track. Much appreciation goes to Briony Grogan, in publicity, and to Martin Hughes and Tom Masters, my fellow authors on LP's *London* city guide (Martin, one day I'm going to get you back for 'certifiably groovy'!) Finally, on a much more sombre note, I'd like to dedicate this book to my father, Tony, who died – without ever again seeing his birthplace, England – while it was being written.

The 1st and 2nd editions of this book were written by Steve Fallon.

PHOTOGRAPHER

Neil Setchfield

Welsh-born Neil Setchfield has worked as a full-time travel photographer for the past 15 years. His work has appeared in over 100 newspapers and magazines throughout the world, as well as in food- and guidebooks. In his spare time he drinks beer and laughs a lot – not always at the same time.

SEND US YOUR FEEDBACK

We love to hear from travellers – your comments keep us on our toes and help make our books better. Our well-travelled team reads every word on what you loved or loathed about this book. Although we cannot reply individually to postal submissions, we always guarantee that your feedback goes straight to the appropriate authors, in time for the next edition – and the most useful submissions are rewarded with a free book. To send us your updates – and find out about LP events, newsletters and travel news – visit our award-winning website: 🖳 www.lonelyplanet.com.

Note: We may edit, reproduce and incorporate your comments in Lonely Planet products such as guidebooks, websites and digital products, so let us know if you don't want your comments reproduced or your name acknowledged. For a copy of our privacy policy visit 🖳 www.lonelyplanet.com/privacy.

Lonely Planet books provide independent advice. Lonely Planet does not accept advertising in guidebooks, nor do we accept payment in exchange for listing or endorsing any place or business. Lonely Planet writers do not accept discounts or payments in exchange for positive coverage of any sort.

Introducing London

Welcome to the mother of all tourist destinations. Style gurus might decree something like 'São Paolo is hot right now', but in the garden of world cities, the UK capital is the hardiest of perennials.

As the home to Big Ben, the British Museum, Kew Gardens, the National Gallery, St Paul's Cathedral, the Tower of London and Westminster Abbey, London never needs a temporary accolade from well-meaning EU bureaucrats. It's a European capital of culture every year.

Like any living thing that's taken root on the planet, London has good and bad seasons. But recently it's been blooming. Millennium projects such as Tate Modern, the London Eye and the (once wobbly) Millennium Bridge have opened up new vistas from the revamped South Bank of the Thames. The city has suddenly embraced bold modern architecture, as in the gherkin-shaped Swiss Re Tower now on the skyline, and a planned shard-of-glass tower at London Bridge. And, with the made-over Trafalgar Square and South Bank, it's started to rediscover its public spaces.

Not only have decently priced and designer hotels sprung up; a new generation of restaurants means Londoners are enjoying their first decent meal out in years. Such is the quality of theatre here that Hollywood stars have been willing to perform for the minimum wage, and even the clubbing scene – always buzzing – has been on a high.

Tolerant and multicultural London might be, but it can be brusque, impersonal and chaotic, too. Things aren't all rosy. In one of those eye-catching new buildings – the glass-walled City Hall – the mayor has been working hard to solve the capital's obdurate problems: a decrepit transport system, filthy streets, inequality of wealth…and trying to win the 2012 Olympic bid. However, just having a mayor again (see p105) has refuelled the city's confidence and put London well and truly back on the map.

As if it ever went away.

Eye-catching sculpture outside the British Museum

Neighbourhoods

Whoever said that London was a collection of villages drew the city map for eternity; the British capital is, and long will be, a patchwork of unique neighbourhoods. Although many Londoners might find themselves having to commute across town for work, they tend to socialise, shop and entertain themselves in the areas where their homes and friends are located.

CENTRAL LONDON

The so-called **West End** is London's epicentre, but parts of it typify what people dislike about the entire city. The main thoroughfare, Oxford St, is as congested and clogged up with debris as any sclerotic artery. More pleasant to explore are the backstreets of restaurant-heavy **Soho** and boutique-shop mecca, **Covent Garden**.

North of Oxford St lie the TV-production stronghold of **Fitzrovia** ('Noho') and literary **Bloomsbury**. To the southwest are the affluent **Mayfair** and **St James's**, which are home to some of the capital's most luxurious hotels. **Westminster**, even further south, is the seat of government. **Marylebone** and **Edgware Road**, north of Oxford St, have been nicknamed 'Little Beirut' for their preponderance of Lebanese and other Middle Eastern restaurants and cafés.

> ### Off the Beaten Track
> It is possible to avoid the crowds in this populous city. The following are little-known gems that many Londoners haven't even visited:
> - Chelsea Physic Garden (p36)
> - City Farms (p41)
> - Dennis Severs' House (p39)
> - Dulwich Picture Gallery (p32)
> - Eltham Palace (p38)
> - Geffrye Museum (p30)
> - Old Operating Theatre (p39)
> - Wallace Collection (p33)

The toe-curling Old Operating Theatre

WEST LONDON

The received wisdom is that north London (see below) is home to the literati, while west London has the glitterati. The area from **South Kensington** to Notting Hill is where you'll find major stars such as Madonna and Hugh Grant and the capital's 'It' girls.

Of course, it's the inner west that remains the most posh. Serious money, nobility and the ghost of the 1980s Sloane Ranger still stalk **Chelsea** and **Knightsbridge**.

Notting Hill isn't quite on the same level. But, once home to a working-class Afro-Caribbean community, it has become seriously upmarket in recent years. Its bohemian chic attracts many 'trustafarians' (trust-fund Rastafarians, or privileged young things seeking a bit of street cred). **Bayswater** and **Westbourne Grove** fall roughly into the Notting Hill mould.

NORTH LONDON

In certain sectors of Britain's scurrilous tabloid press, the name **Hampstead** is virtually synonymous with 'the chattering classes' or liberal intellectuals, while upper middle-class **Islington** is resonant of Tony Blair's 'new Labour' project. (Also, the Blair family's home before No 10 was in Islington.)

On the streets, Hampstead's proximity to the expansive heath has made it one of London's most pleasant locations and expensive real estate areas, alongside the equally leafy and affluent **Highgate**. Islington's Upper St has gone from being lined with interesting bars to being largely overrun with chain pubs. Today, a few gems remain but **Stoke Newington** to the north has a bit more 'edge'.

Camden, with its celebrated market, is a bit like an Oxford St of the north, albeit full of more alternative types. Nearby **Primrose Hill**, with its younger film stars and fashionistas is definitely more chichi.

EAST LONDON

Large swathes of working-class east London have undergone a renaissance in the last decade. First, penniless artists homed in on **Hoxton** and **Shoreditch** in the early 1990s for affordable urban living. About five years later, affluent workers in the neighbouring **City of London** or 'Square Mile' – London's financial hub – became aware of this district on their doorstep. Today, Hoxton and Shoreditch still house some of the capital's best bars and clubs, but many of the artists who originally colonised it have had to move further east to **Hackney**.

Clerkenwell and **Farringdon**, home to the *Guardian* newspaper and other media, have also been regenerated, with architects and other creative businesses moving in.

Brick Lane is lined with curry houses, but its displays of multi-ethnicity seem a little touristy these days; **Whitechapel** is more of the real deal.

Built in the 1980s, the secondary financial centre of the **Docklands** is a world unto itself – a capitalist theme park worth visiting simply because it's so blimmin' surreal.

SOUTH LONDON

'Sarf' (south) London gets a bad rap. The idea that it's bleaker and offers less to do has been successfully propagated by – guess who? – north Londoners. But this isn't really true.

Clapham, with its huge common and trendy bar-restaurants, has long been a flag-bearer for south London style. Colourful and exotic **Brixton**, which became a focus of Caribbean immigration after WWII, is becoming gentrified, too.

However, the greatest revelation in perhaps all of London has been the makeover of the Thames' **South Bank** in recent years. With the opening of Tate Modern, the Millennium Wheel, Saatchi Gallery, the rebuilt Globe Theatre, Oxo Tower and other restaurants, it's now one of the best places to go in town.

Camden's crammed-to-the-gills market

Itineraries

You could spend years in London and still not see all the capital has to offer. Fortunately, most of the major sights are clustered together, either in Westminster, on the South Bank, in the West End, Bloomsbury or the City of London. The museums, palaces, gardens and other attractions listed here are all must-sees, peppered with a few local favourites.

Some attractions (such as the Tower of London and the British Museum) can get very crowded, especially in summer. Avoid long queues by visiting early in the morning or late in the afternoon and buy tickets in advance from a tourist information centre (TIC) or some Underground stations. If time is tight try these options.

DAY ONE

Visit Westminster Abbey, view Big Ben and the Houses of Parliament, then walk across Westminster Bridge to the London Eye (book for a ride). Stroll along the South Bank, past the Saatchi Gallery, Royal Festival Hall and Hayward Gallery to Tate Modern. After visiting the latter, cross the Millennium Bridge to St Paul's Cathedral, pausing mid-river to take in the magnificent views. In the evening take in a play or dance performance.

Lowlights
Some of the things we could do without (or at least with less of):
- the Underground's run-down state
- garbage bags on Soho's streets
- soulless 'Leachers' (Leicester) Square
- cacophonous London Trocadero
- cabbies' rants about the 'terrible' congestion charge
- the *Daily Mail's* campaign against asylum seekers
- traffic lights that stay green for 17 seconds (and red for 1½ minutes)

DAY TWO

Start at Trafalgar Square and visit the National Gallery or the National Portrait Gallery. Then go to Covent Garden for some elbow-to-elbow window-shopping (explore the backstreets). Stop for a pint in the Salisbury pub on St Martin's Lane, then visit the Photographers' Gallery or the British Museum. Hit a few Hoxton and Shoreditch bars in the evening.

DAY THREE

Visit one of South Kensington's museums (the Victoria & Albert, Natural History or Science). Kensington Palace and the Serpentine Gallery, in the middle of Hyde Park, are both only a short distance away. Alternatively, go up Brompton Rd towards Hyde Park Corner and walk along Constitution Hill to take in the view of Buckingham Palace.

Times & Charges
Mostly, hours listed in the book are the literal opening and closing times. Last admission to most venues is at least 30 minutes before closing time. In the few royal palaces where last entry is well before closing time, we've listed last entry.

Most of London's finest museums and galleries have free admission. However, funding remains a problem, so there are donation boxes (£2 or £3 requested) at many entrances. Special exhibits may incur a separate entrance fee. Keen sightseers should check out the London Pass, which allows free admission to over 50 museums and other attractions.

Highlights

TATE MODERN (3, G4)

Likening it to a shopping centre, celebrated London architect Will Alsop made waves in 2003 when he said he didn't like Tate Modern. He's one of very few, because nearly five million visitors a year have turned this remodelled power station into Europe's most successful contemporary art gallery.

It's not just the world-class art collection that people come to see, either. Swiss architects Pierre de Meuron and Jacques Herzog have transformed the brown-brick building into an aesthetic beacon, with its **central chimney** and new, **glassed-in upper storeys** facing St Paul's across the Thames. Before the 2000 opening, the vast **Turbine Hall** of the disused Bankside Power Station was reworked as a dramatic entrance and exhibition space. Lifts and escalators were installed to take art lovers up to the exhibits.

From the outset these exhibits have been arranged by theme, rather than chronologically or by artist. Works by Georges Braque, Henri Matisse, Roy Lichtenstein, Jackson Pollock, Mark Rothko, Andy Warhol and others are slotted into galleries focusing on either **landscape**, **still life**, **society** or the **body**.

INFORMATION
- ☎ 7887 8008 (recorded information), 7887 8888 (tickets)
- 💻 www.tate.org.uk
- ✉ Bankside SE1
- £ free, £2 donation requested
- 🕙 10am-6pm Sun-Thu, 10am-10pm Fri-Sat
- ℹ audioguide (£1); free tours 11am, noon, 1pm, 2pm, 3pm & 6.30pm
- ⊖ Southwark
- ♿ excellent
- 🍴 Tate Modern cafés L4 & L7

DON'T MISS
- Mark Rothko's murals
- Auguste Rodin's *The Kiss*
- Bill Viola's *Five Angels for the Millennium*
- Picasso's *Girl in a Chemise*
- Sam Taylor-Wood's *Still Life*
- the Turbine Hall

A café on the 4th floor and a café-restaurant on the 7th offer panoramic views and have helped this relative newcomer edge out the venerable British Museum as London's number-one attraction. Such success, coupled with architecture's prestigious Pritzker Prize (2000), is hard to argue with. So if you can't beat 'em, perhaps join 'em, Will?

Tate Modern's towering Turbine Hall: once an old power station, now a stunning art space

BRITISH MUSEUM (3, D3)

The UK's largest museum is very much one of antiquity and of empire, with vast **Egyptian**, **Etruscan**, **Greek**, **Oriental** and **Roman galleries**, among others. The collections have certainly grown since royal physician Hans Sloane (of Sloane Square fame) inaugurated them by selling his 'cabinet of curiosities' to the nation in 1753. The most recent, 21st-century additions are the **Wellcome Gallery of Ethnography** and the **Sainsbury African Galleries**.

The latter is in the inner courtyard, which was famously renovated by Sir Norman Foster for the new millennium; the light-filled **Great Court** is now covered with a spectacular glass-and-steel roof instead of being hidden from the public as it was for 150 years. At the museum's heart lies the Great Court, with the fabulous **Reading Room** of the old British Library, where George Bernard Shaw and Mahatma Gandhi studied and Karl Marx wrote *The Communist Manifesto*.

INFORMATION

- ☎ 7323 8000
- 🖥 www.thebritishmus eum.ac.uk
- ✉ Great Russell St WC1
- £ free, donations appreciated; prices vary for special exhibitions
- 🕙 10am-5.30pm, to 8.30pm Thu-Fri (selected galleries only)
- ℹ Highlights audio-guide £3.50 (90min); highlights tours (90min) 10.30am, 1pm & 3pm £8/5; free Eye Opener tours (50-60min) 11am-3.30pm
- ⊖ Tottenham Court Rd/Russell Sq
- ♿ good
- ✗ Court Café, Gallery Café, Court Restaurant

DON'T MISS

- Egyptian mummies
- Parthenon Marbles
- Oxus Treasure
- Rosetta Stone
- Sutton Hoo Treasure

Great Court, with its soaring glass canopy

Before stepping foot into any part of the museum, however, be prepared for its size and popularity. The best thing is to choose exactly what you want to see, as you can't cover much of the collections in one day. (Remember, admission is free so you can come back several times.) If you want to avoid the crowds at the imposing porticoed main entrance off Great Russell St, try the back entrance off Montague Place.

Another thing this well-stocked museum houses is controversy. In the run-up to the 2004 Athens Olympics, Greece stepped up its campaign for the return of the **Parthenon Marbles**, shipped to England by British ambassador Lord Elgin in 1806. However, successive Greek governments have been requesting the marbles' return for years.

BRITISH AIRWAYS LONDON EYE   (3, E5)

On a clear day from the world's largest Ferris wheel you can see 25 miles (40km) in every direction – as far as Windsor to the west and, to the east, nearly out to sea. But it's not just its size and range that make the 135m-tall London Eye so immensely appealing. The 32 glass-enclosed gondolas glide slowly and gracefully as the wheel takes 30 minutes to rotate completely, so passengers (up to 25 in each capsule) really get time to take in the magnificent view.

Built to celebrate the new millennium, the wheel had an embarrassingly delayed start, as New Year's Eve 1999 rolled around long before it ever did. Now it's hard to imagine **Jubilee Gardens** and the Thames South Bank without this much-loved icon. Instead of being removed in 2005 as originally intended, it's staying put until at least 2028, giving the riverside an uplifting, carnival feel.

You can buy tickets from the office behind the wheel. However, the queues get very long, so arrive very early, or better still, book ahead. You still need to arrive 30 minutes before your 'flight' to pick up advance tickets. Special romantic and champagne packages are available.

INFORMATION

- ☎ 0870 500 0600
- 🖥 www.ba-londoneye.com
- ✉ Jubilee Gardens SE1
- £ £11.50/5.50-10, 5% discount for online bookings
- 🕙 9.30am-8pm, to 9pm or 10pm on weekends in May, Jun & Sep, to 10pm Jul & Aug, closed 5-31 Jan
- ⊖ Waterloo
- ♿ excellent
- ✗ People's Palace at Royal Festival Hall (p75)

London's Bridges

London has 15 bridges between the neo-Gothic Tower Bridge in the east and Battersea Bridge in the southwest. The one with the longest history is London Bridge, linking Southwark and the City (though today's incarnation dates from as recently as 1972). The most beautiful is the Millennium Bridge, between Bankside and the City, which proved to have a bad case of the wobbles when it opened in June 2000 and had to close for repairs before reopening in late 2002. The newest 'opening' has been of 2003's Golden Jubilee Bridge, a refurbishment of, addition to and rebranding of the Hungerford Bridge between Waterloo and Charing Cross.

Get a bird's-eye view from the London Eye

WESTMINSTER ABBEY (3, D6)

The site of coronations and royal burials, and the well from which the Anglican church draws its inspiration, Westminster Abbey has long been pivotal to English history. There's been an abbey on this site since at least the 11th century under Edward the Confessor, and possibly even longer. Edward, later beatified, remains here, buried in the chapel behind the main altar, not far from the **Coronation Chair**, where almost every monarch since the late 13th century has been crowned.

Often described as the best example of early English Gothic, the abbey is a mix of architectural styles. In the 13th century, Henry III began enlarging Edward's abbey, and this work continued for centuries. The tall, French Gothic nave was not completed until 1388, **Henry VII's Chapel** was added in 1519, and in the mid-18th century two towers were built by Christopher Wren and his pupil Nicholas Hawksmoor above the exit (west door).

Royals buried in Henry VII's Chapel (also known as the Lady Chapel) include Henry VII, Elizabeth I and the two princes murdered in the tower (see p15). In the southern transept, across from the main door is **Poets' Corner**, where Geoffrey Chaucer, Edmund Spenser, Ben and Samuel Johnson, Alfred Lord Tennyson and others are buried.

Separate museums around the **cloister** are the **Chapter House**, the **Abbey Museum** and the **Pyx Chamber**, once the Royal Treasury.

The most atmospheric way to experience the abbey is to attend an **evensong** service. Otherwise, be aware that you'll be joining huge, thronging crowds. Coming early or late is always a good idea.

INFORMATION

- ☎ 7654 4900 or 7222 5152
- ▢ www.westminster-abbey.org
- ✉ Dean's Yard SW1
- £ £7.50/5, family £15
- ☷ 9.30am-3.45pm Mon-Fri, to 7pm Thu, 9am-1.45pm Sat, evensong 5pm Mon-Fri, 3pm Sat-Sun
- ⓘ audioguide (£3); 1½hr tours (£4), 3-6 per day
- ⊖ Westminster
- ♿ good
- ✗ Westminster Arms

DON'T MISS

- College Garden
- Poets' Corner
- Queen Elizabeth's tomb
- Quire (chancel) tomb of Mary Queen of Scots

HOUSES OF PARLIAMENT (3, D6)

Portrayed in oils by Monet and Turner and depicted on millions of post-cards, the Palace of Westminster is a landmark that even first-time visitors find eerily familiar. This ornate Victorian-Gothic confection overshadowing the Thames certainly lives up to its status as the home of one of the world's oldest parliaments, dating from the mid-13th century.

Designed by Charles Barry and Augustus Pugin in 1840 after a devastating fire, the current building is most famous for its chiming clock tower, commonly known as **Big Ben**. However, many visitors also like to see inside the Houses of Parliament (the **House of Commons** and the **House of Lords**).

There are two ways of doing this. When Parliament is sitting (all year except for recesses at Easter, Christmas and three months in summer), you can watch from the visitors' galleries as politicians heckle one another below. (Queues are much longer to the Strangers' Gallery in the Commons than the House of Lords visitors' gallery.) Otherwise, guided tours are held in summer. Security is always very tight.

House of Commons

Based on St Stephen's Chapel in the original Palace of Westminster, the current chamber, redesigned by Giles Gilbert Scott after WWII, replaced an earlier version destroyed in 1941. Although the Commons is a national assembly of 659 members of Parliament (MPs), the chamber only seats 437. Government members sit to the right of the Speaker, the opposition to the left. The House Speaker presides over business from a chair donated by Australia, while ministers speak from a despatch box given by New Zealand.

INFORMATION

- ☎ 7219 4272 (House of Commons Information Office), 7219 3107 (House of Lords Information Office)
- 🖥 www.parliament.uk
- ✉ Parliament Sq SW1 (visitors: St Stephen's Entrance, St Margaret St SW1)
- £ free
- ☺ when Parliament is sitting – Commons 2.30-10.30pm Mon, 11.30am-7pm Tue-Wed, 11.30am-6.30pm Thu, 9.30am-3pm Fri; Lords 2.30-10pm Mon-Wed, 11am-1.30pm & 3-7.30pm Thu, 11am-3pm Fri
- ⓘ guided 1¼hr tours (☎ 0870 906 3773) 9.30am-3.30pm Mon-Sat late Jul-late Sep, £7/5, family £22
- ⊖ Westminster
- ♿ good
- ✕ Westminster Arms

Left of the security area is the stunning hammer-beam roof (dating from 1401) of **Westminster Hall** (1099). This is the oldest surviving part of the Palace of Westminster, the seat of English monarchy in the Middle Ages. The hall was also used as a sometime courthouse and the trials of William Wallace (1305), Sir Thomas More (1535), Guy Fawkes (1606) and Charles I (1649) took place here.

The tower at the opposite end of the palace to Big Ben is Victoria Tower (1860).

NATIONAL GALLERY (6, C3)

The UK's foremost art collection is presented very formally, with gilt-framed classical paintings hung in huge vaulted halls. The relative hush among its parquet flooring and embossed wallpaper does give it a slightly paternalistic, 'eat-your-greens' tone…but then, we figure, those greens *are* good for you.

More than 2000 paintings form a **continuous timeline**, from the old masters (1260–1510) in the Sainsbury Wing addition and the Renaissance-influenced West Wing (1510–1600) to the Dutch- and Italian-focused North Wing (1600–1700) and East Wing (1700–1900). However, to attempt to follow this timeline in one dutiful take would clearly be exhausting.

So it's fortunate that the gallery's quality leaps out as much as its size. You can cherry-pick, heading for Vermeer's *Young Woman Standing at a Virginal* (Room 16), Rembrandt's *Woman Bathing in a Stream* (Room 23) or Seurat's *Bathers at Asnières* (Room 44). Whether you're sticking to must-sees or seeking personal favourites, picking up a **free floor plan** is essential. Among other works on display are paintings by Canaletto, Caravaggio, Gainsborough, Monet, Raphael, Renoir, Titian and Turner. Among such heavy hitters, Room 17a's **Hoogstraten's Peepshow**, which creates a 3-D illusion, provides some light relief.

INFORMATION

- ☎ 7747 2885
- 🖥 www.nationalgallery .org.uk
- ✉ Trafalgar Sq WC2
- £ free
- 🕑 10am-6pm, to 9pm Wed
- ℹ audioguide (£4 requested; deposit, usually a passport, required); 1hr tours 11.30am & 2.30pm, plus 6.30pm Wed
- ⊖ Charing Cross/ Leicester Sq
- ♿ good
- ✗ Gallery Café, Sainsbury Wing restaurant

DON'T MISS

- Van Gogh's *Sunflowers*
- Constable's *The Hay Wain*
- Velázquez's *Rokeby Venus*
- Van Eyck's *Arnolfini Portrait*
- Da Vinci's *The Virgin and Child with St Anne and St John the Baptist* cartoon
- *The Wilton Diptych*

Founded in the 19th century, the National Gallery most recently embarked on a refurbishment in 2003–04 to create a courtyard and new entrances from the revamped Trafalgar Square. The designs have not raised the sort of controversy surrounding the 1980s **Sainsbury Wing**, when conservative-minded Prince Charles dismissed the form proposed as a 'carbuncle'. The Sainsbury Wing was eventually re-designed by different architects.

Go cherry-picking at the National Gallery

TOWER OF LONDON (3, J4)

'Uneasy lies the head that wears the crown' – that Shakespearean quote comes quickly to mind when you're visiting the Tower of London. After all, King Henry VIII's wife Anne Boleyn was one queen beheaded here in the 16th century. Today it's where you'll find the British **Crown Jewels**.

Begun in 1078 during the reign of William the Conqueror, this well-preserved castle complex is one of London's three World Heritage Sites (beside Westminster Abbey and Maritime Greenwich). The **White Tower** at its heart was the original building. Walls, more towers, a riverside wharf and a palace were added over the next few centuries.

Originally a royal residence, the tower was increasingly used as a prison after Henry VIII relocated to Whitehall Palace in 1529. Sir Thomas More, Lady Jane Grey and Princess (later Queen) Elizabeth were all held captive here. You can see the **Queen's House** where Anne Boleyn was imprisoned before her execution on the nearby scaffold site, plus the infamous **Bloody Tower**, where Edward V and his brother were allegedly murdered, possibly by their uncle, Richard III. The tower's modern history is less gruesome, although the last prisoner – Nazi Rudolf Hess – didn't leave until the 1940s.

With more than two million visitors a year, the trick is to buy your ticket from any London Underground station and go in the afternoon.

INFORMATION

- ☎ 0870 756 6060 (information), 0870 756 7070 (tickets)
- 💻 www.hrp.org.uk
- ✉ Tower Hill EC3
- £ £13.50/8-10.50, family £37.50, £1 discount for prebooking
- ☾ 9am-6pm Tue-Sat, 10am-6pm Sun-Mon Mar-Oct, to 5pm Nov-Feb
- ⓘ audioguide (£3); free 1hr Beefeater tours every 30min 9.30am-3.30pm (from 10am Sun-Mon, to 2.30pm Nov-Feb)
- ⊖ Tower Hill
- ♿ fair
- ✕ Café Spice Namaste (p70)

Ravens & Beefeaters

Legend has it that should the ravens fly away, the White Tower will crumble and a great disaster will befall England. So the Tudor-costumed Yeoman Warders (Beefeaters) guarding the tower take the safe option and clip the birds' wings. But why Beefeaters? In the 17th century the guards received a daily ration of beer and beef, a luxury well beyond the reach of the poor. And so the envious nickname was born.

NATIONAL PORTRAIT GALLERY (6, D3)

Compared to the sometimes overawing National Gallery, the NPG is simply lots of fun. It's possibly unique in being a gallery where the subjects are more important than the art, and its 10,000 portraits of Britain's great and good down the ages gives credence to Thomas Carlyle's notion that history is little but 'the biography of great men' (and women).

Recent renovations have reordered the collection, with pictures now ranging chronologically from the top floor to the bottom. An escalator takes you directly to the top floor, where you'll find **classical portraits** of Richard III, Henry VIII, Elizabeth I, Shakespeare and the Stuart kings.

From here the collection snakes down towards the 21st century, passing self-portraits of **Hogarth** and **Reynolds**, pictures of Prime Ministers Gladstone and Disraeli and numerous captains of sea and industry. There's an area devoted to the **Romantic poets** such as Keats, Byron and Shelley, at which point you might start to wonder whether portrait painters of yore followed a template, adjusting it only slightly to accommodate individuals' features.

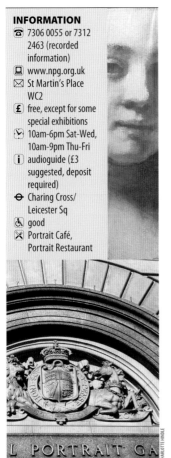

Put faces to the famous at the NPG

CHARLOTTE HINDLE

INFORMATION

- ☎ 7306 0055 or 7312 2463 (recorded information)
- 🖳 www.npg.org.uk
- ✉ St Martin's Place WC2
- £ free, except for some special exhibitions
- ☽ 10am-6pm Sat-Wed, 10am-9pm Thu-Fri
- ⓘ audioguide (£3 suggested, deposit required)
- ⊖ Charing Cross/ Leicester Sq
- ♿ good
- ✗ Portrait Café, Portrait Restaurant

DON'T MISS

Portraits of William Shakespeare, Henry VIII, Queen Elizabeth I, Oliver Cromwell, Lord Byron, Lady Emma Hamilton, Charles Darwin, Winston Churchill, TE Lawrence and Diana, Princess of Wales

The collection is rotated, so not all works are on show at any one time. However, by the time you get to the **Balcony Gallery** on the 1st floor, you'll be among such recent sitters as Prime Minister Harold Wilson, poet Philip Larkin and trade union leader Arthur Scargill. The ground floor is the most popular, with photos by celebrity photographers such as Mario Testino (of Naomi Campbell, Kate Moss et al fame) mixed with sculptures and paintings of **modern-day celebrities**.

An **IT Gallery** on the mezzanine above the information desk lets you look at the entire collection – including the archive – digitally. June to September is when to see entrants in the highly regarded BP Portrait Award.

MADAME TUSSAUD'S (3, A2)

Madame Tussaud's polarises opinion. For the three million or so annual visitors who propel it into the list of London's top 10 sights, it rules. Strangely enough, though, millions of others on the planet seem quite happy to skip this leading waxworks museum.

So if you've already inked this sight into your itinerary, you probably won't be deterred. Otherwise, may we suggest the National Portrait Gallery (see opposite) as a better examination of celebrity?

As you emerge from the lifts (elevators) you're met by an interactive mural of shouting paparazzi, which pretty much sets the tone for the **Garden Party** exhibition, featuring models of celebrities du jour 'mingling' with tourists. Party 'guests' are rotated, but there's a corner where a professional photographer will take your photo with, say, Julia Roberts or the rubber-foam-bottomed Brad Pitt.

Below, in the **Grand Hall** there's a menagerie of world leaders and sportspeople throughout history,

> **INFORMATION**
> ☎ 0870 400 3000
> 🖥 www.madame
> -tussauds.com
> ✉ Marylebone Rd NW1
> £ prices vary according to time of entry: adult £12-22, concession £7-17
> ⊙ 9am-5.30pm Jun–mid-Sep, 10am-5.30pm Mon-Fri, 9.30am-5.30pm Sat-Sun mid-Sep–May
> ⊖ Baker St
> ♿ good
> ✗ Costa Coffee

plus a stage where you can play *Pop Idol (American Idol)*. The following **Chamber of Horrors** is laughably undisturbing and the **Spirit of London** 'time taxi', a funfair-type ride where you sit in a mock-up of a London black cab and are whipped through a five-minute summary of the city's history, is simply cringeworthy. ('After the Battle of Trafalgar, Lord Nelson kept one eye on the celebrations', runs one god-awful line of commentary as you pass Nelson and his eye patch.)

It might be easier to treat this all as a bit of a laugh, were it not for the hefty prices and the lengthy queues. (Beat the latter by paying extra for a timed entry slot.) Then again, if you love a bit of kitsch, this place might be for you.

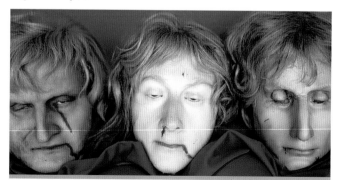

Hang with the hapless residents of Madame Tussaud's Chamber of Horrors

SHAKESPEARE'S GLOBE (3, G4)

Boo! Hiss! Heckle the actors! See Shakespeare as it was performed orginally! The rebuilt Globe is no ordinary theatre and you're welcome to do all those things here. This faithful replica of the original 'Wooden O' has the same central stage left open to the elements, surrounded by a roofed ring of seats. It also uses Elizabethan construction methods and materials and is only 200 metres from the original Globe Theatre, where Shakespeare worked from 1599 to 1611.

Most importantly, however, performers remain true to the Bard's essentially populist nature. Men often play women and all the actors are up close and personal with the audience, the nearest 500 of whom stand in the stalls. Stage lighting and sound systems are eschewed.

The building's structure means viewers need to be well prepared

Wanamaker's Dream

Closed by the Puritans in 1642, who regarded theatres as dens of iniquity, the Globe was just a historical footnote when American actor/director Sam Wanamaker came searching for it in 1949. The original theatre's foundations had vanished beneath a row of listed Georgian houses, but Wanamaker was undeterred. He set up the Globe Playhouse Trust in 1970 and began fundraising for a memorial theatre to be built nearby. Work started in 1987. Sadly, Wanamaker died four years before the new Globe opened in 1997.

Join cross-dressers and hecklers at the Globe

for the elements, not to mention the planes flying overhead and a potentially restricted view due to two 'authentic' Corinthian pillars. At least in winter, performances move indoors to the Jacobean-style **Inigo Jones Theatre** next door.

If you can't catch *Richard III* or *The Taming of the Shrew* for example, you can walk the boards and learn about the Globe's history with a daytime guided tour of the theatre and the marvellous exhibition of Elizabethan London below. Particularly interesting are the displays devoted to Elizabethan special effects.

INFORMATION

- ☎ 7902 1500 (exhibition), 7401 9919 (theatre tickets)
- 🖳 www.shakespeares -globe.org
- ✉ 21 New Globe Walk SE1
- £ exhibition £8/5.50-6.50, family £24; theatre seats £11-29; standing room £5
- 🕙 9am-noon (exhibition & theatre tour) plus 12.30-5pm (exhibition) May-Sep, 10am-5pm (exhibition & theatre tour) Oct-Apr, 7.30pm (performances) May-Sep
- ⊖ Southwark/London Bridge
- ♿ good
- ✕ Globe Café, Globe Restaurant

ST PAUL'S CATHEDRAL (3, G3)

A dome, a whole lot of stairs and a view: that could be one Hollywood-style high-concept summation of the typical tourist experience of architect Sir Christopher Wren's *tour de force*. But to Londoners the landmark St Paul's Cathedral resonates more as the home of important state occasions, from Winston Churchill's funeral to the wedding of Charles and Lady Di. Built after the Great Fire of London and inaugurated in 1697, the cathedral's survival during the London Blitz of WWII made it a symbol of British grit.

Major interior renovations are due to be completed by 2005, but exterior cleaning will continue until 2008. Throughout, however, it will remain possible to climb the 530 steps inside London's largest **church dome** to the **Whispering**, **Stone** and **Golden Galleries**. Climbing at least as far as the Stone Gallery (378 steps) offers panoramic views.

Inside the cathedral are ornately carved **choir stalls** by Grinling Gibbons, **iron gates** by Jean Tijou, Holman Hunt's *Light of the World* and an **effigy of John Donne**, author of the immortal line 'No man is an island' and one-time dean of St Paul's. Around the altar, with its gilded oak canopy, is the **American Chapel**, a memorial to 28,000 American expats killed in WWII.

The floor below the dome bears a compass design with Wren's epitaph: *Lector, si monumentum requiris, circumspice* (Reader, if you seek his monument, look around you). Actually, though, Wren's monument is in the **crypt**, where he's buried along with the Duke of Wellington, General Kitchener and Lord Nelson.

From 2004, the redevelopment of Paternoster Square surrounding St Paul's will see Wren's **Temple Bar** (1669), London's only surviving city gate, returned after 125 years.

St Paul's magnificent mosaic ceiling

INFORMATION

☎ 7236 4128
🖥 www.stpauls.co.uk
✉ St Paul's Churchyard EC4
£ £6/3-5
🕑 8.30am-5pm Mon-Sat, evensong 5pm most weekdays, 3.15pm Sun
ℹ 45min audioguide (£3.50/3); 90min guided tours (£2.50/1-2), 4 daily
⊖ St Paul's
♿ good
🍴 Crypt Café, Refectory Restaurant

TATE BRITAIN (2, E5)

While its younger sibling, Tate Modern (p9) has stolen much of its thunder, Tate Britain has been quietly strengthening its role as an archive of British art from the 16th century to today. Shipping works of international contemporary art down the river to its Bankside sister and opening new exhibition spaces in 2000 have given this Millbank gallery more room to breathe.

INFORMATION

☎ 7887 8008 (recorded information), 7887 8888 (tickets)

▯ www.tate.org.uk

✉ Millbank SW1

£ free

⏱ 10am-5.50pm

⊖ Pimlico

♿ excellent

✗ Tate Café & Espresso Bar, Tate Britain Restaurant

Sir John Millais, artist in residence

Works by **Constable** and **William Blake**, in particular, have had extra space dedicated to them and, with a decade-old rotation system still in place, rooms have been temporarily given over in the past few years to the likes of Aubrey Beardsley, Terry Frost, William Hogarth, Henry Moore and Stanley Spencer.

The original Tate Gallery was founded on this site in 1897 by sugar magnate Sir Henry Tate, and as befits such a museum of historical record, the collection largely remains in chronological order. However, within that overall organisation you will find certain themes. For example, there's a section on Art and Victorian Society, while 1980s British Sculpture contains works by Antony Gormley and Anish Kapoor.

Other artists on show in the main building include Francis Bacon, Lucian Freud, David Hockney and Victorian racehorse-fancier George Stubbs. There's a **Gainsborough Octagon**, while the huge Turner collection is in the postmodern annexe of the **Clore Gallery**.

Finally, Tate Britain steals the thunder back from its modern sister every December, when it hosts the controversial **Turner Prize** of contemporary British art.

Tate-à-Tate

If you wish to see both of London's Tate galleries, Britain and Modern, you can easily travel between the two in style. The **Tate-to-Tate** boat – which sports a Damien Hirst dot painting – will whisk you from the Millennium Pier at Tate Britain to the Bankside Pier at Tate Modern, stopping en route at the London Eye. Services run from 10am to 6pm daily, at 40-minute intervals. Tickets are available from either Tate Modern or Tate Britain and cost £3.40 for a single or £5 for a day pass. When tidal requirements dictate, a replacement boat may be used.

KEW GARDENS (1, B1)

The Royal Botanic Gardens at Kew give a whole new meaning to the term 'greenhouse effect': their famous metal-and-glass **Palm House** (1844–48), and other hothouses lure one million visitors a year. Kew's 120-hectare expanse of lawns, formal gardens and parkland are especially popular during spring and summer, but it's these climate-controlled conservatories that make a visit worthwhile in any season.

The Palm House, near the main Victoria Gate, is home to exotic tropical greenery. There's a tiny **Water Lily House** (open March to December) to the northwest, and further north lies the **Princess of Wales Conservatory** (1985), with plants in 10 different computer-controlled climate zones. It's here you find the most famous of Kew's 38,000 plant species, the 2m-tall **Titan Arum**, or corpse flower, which is overpoweringly obnoxious-smelling when it blooms.

Other highlights include the **Temperate House**, **Kew Palace** (built in 1631) and **Queen Charlotte's Cottage**, the latter two popular with 'mad' King George III and his wife, Charlotte. Don't forget to see the **Japanese Gateway** and the celebrated **Great Pagoda** (1761), designed by William Chambers. The Marianne North Gallery and the Kew Gardens Gallery feature paintings on a botanical theme, while Museum No 1 demonstrates how plant materials have been fashioned into clothes, medicines and implements.

If this Unesco World Heritage Site seems too vast, the **Kew Explorer** minitrain (£3.50/1.50) will whizz you around in 40 minutes.

INFORMATION

- ☎ 8332 5655/5000
- 🖥 www.rbgkew.org.uk
- ✉ Kew Rd, Kew, Surrey
- £ £8.50/6; late entry (45min before hothouses closes) £6
- 🕙 gardens 9.30am-dusk; glasshouses 9.30am-5.30pm Apr-Sep, 9.30am-5pm Oct & Feb-Mar, 9.30am-4.15pm Nov-Jan
- ⊖ Kew Gardens
- 🚢 from Westminster Pier (1½hr) up to 5 per day late Mar-Sep/Oct (single/return £9/15)
  - ☎ 7930 4721
- 🚻 good
- ✗ The Orangery (p73)

Based on the design of an upturned hull, the Palm House is home to exotic shrubs and palms

KENSINGTON PALACE (2, C4)

Any reader who lived through 1997 will remember Kensington Palace as the residence of Diana, the late princess of Wales. And while the carpet of floral bouquets covering the lawn during that September's emotional, very un-British period of mourning is but a memory, a collection of the princess's attention-grabbing frocks remains. It's still one of this living palace's major draws, forming the highlight of the **Royal Ceremonial Dress Collection**.

Of course, Kensington Palace already had a long history when Diana moved in after her divorce from Prince Charles in 1986. Built in 1605, it became the favourite royal residence under William and Mary of Orange in 1689, and remained so until the death of George I in 1760. Even afterwards the royals stayed occasionally, with Queen Victoria being born here in 1819.

INFORMATION

- ☎ 0870 751 5170 (recorded information), 0870 751 5180 (booking)
- 🖵 www.hrp.org.uk
- ✉ Kensington Palace State Apartments W8
- £ palace £10.80/7-8.20, family £32, £1 discount for prebooking; park & gardens free
- 🕙 palace 10am-6pm Mar-Oct, 10am-5pm Nov-Feb; park & gardens 5am-30min before dusk
- ⓘ audioguide tours are self-paced (about 1½hr)
- ⊖ Queensway/Notting Hill Gate
- ♿ good
- 🍴 The Orangery (p73)

DON'T MISS

- Kent's painting of a two-eyed Cyclops (King's Long Gallery)
- King's Staircase
- Queen Victoria Memorial Room
- Round Pond
- Van Dyck's *Cupid and Venus* (King's Drawing Room)

In the 17th and 18th centuries, Kensington Palace was variously renovated by Sir Christopher Wren and William Kent. So, today you'll find yourself walking through the surprisingly small, wood-panelled State Apartments dating from William's time and the grander apartments by Kent during the Georgian period. Most beautiful is the **Cupola Room**, where the ceremony of initiating men into the exclusive Order of the Garter took place.

The **Sunken Garden** near the palace is prettiest during summer. Nearby is the Orangery, designed by Nicholas Hawksmoor and Vanbrugh with carvings by Grinling Gibbons, and now a tearoom.

Favoured royal pad, Kensington Palace

BUCKINGHAM PALACE (3, B5)

Thanks to *Daily Mirror* reporter Ryan Parry, who worked undercover as a footman for two months, the world has a better idea of how the royal family's private realm appears: pink-and-red flock wallpaper reminiscent of a suburban pub, wooden wall units, beds covered in teddy bears and Tupperware containers at breakfast.

So when Buck Palace throws open its doors to visitors in August and September it's possibly a good thing that only 19 of its 661 rooms are on display. Fortunately, too, these are all staterooms designed for public consumption, where the Queen and her corgis welcome visiting dignitaries such as George W Bush (in cowboy boots) and valiant English rugby teams.

The tours have been run since 1993 as part of a charm offensive to counter increasingly negative press images of the Windsors. Whether the opulence of the **Guard Room**, **State Dining Room**, **Ballroom** and several drawing rooms would win over advocates of a republic is doubtful. Royal fans, however, will certainly be wowed.

There's a hint of private kitsch in the **Throne Room**, where pink,

MANFRED GOTTSCHALK

INFORMATION

☎ 7839 1377 or 7766 7300 (advance bookings)

🖳 www.the-royal -collection.org.uk

✉ The Mall SW1

£ £12.50/6.50-10.50, family £31.50, plus £1 booking fee

🕙 9.30am-4.30pm Aug-Sep

ℹ Changing of the guard 11.30am Apr-Aug, alternate days Sep-Mar (☎ 09068 663344 for exact dates)

⊖ Green Park/St James's Park/Victoria

♿ good

🍴 ICA Cafe (p32)

On Guard!

'They're changing the guard at Buckingham Palace, Christopher Robin went down with Alice.' When even *Winnie the Pooh* author AA Milne has written about the changing of the guard, you can be sure you're observing a quintessential English ceremony. It takes place on the forecourt of Buckingham Palace, where the old watch comes off duty and is replaced by a new one. You need to arrive early to get a decent view of the implacable guards in their bright-red uniforms and bearskin hats.

his-and-hers chairs bear the initials *ER* and *P*. Meanwhile, wonderfully ornate state coaches are found in the adjoining **Royal Mews**.

The renovated **Picture Gallery** is most impressive, with works by Rembrandt, Van Dyck, Canaletto, Poussin and Vermeer – even if you can see similar works at the National Gallery (p14), and for free.

Buckingham House (1705) has been a royal residence since 1837, when Queen Victoria moved in. There's no chance you'll spy the current incumbents – they're far away on their hols well before the industrial-strength carpet is rolled out for the proles.

NATURAL HISTORY MUSEUM (2, C5)

The Natural History Museum is very much a museum of two halves: the **Life Galleries** in the gloriously over-the-top Gothic Revival building approached from Cromwell Rd, and the slick **Earth Galleries**, whose entrance lies around the corner on Exhibition Rd. The only real unifying factor is that both are extremely kid-friendly.

Granted, there are modern additions to the Life Galleries, including **animatronic dinosaurs**, a stunning room on **creepy crawlies** and the vast new **Darwin Centre** (whose 22 million zoological specimens are seen by tour). Yet architect Alfred Waterhouse's 19th-century building still overwhelmingly evokes the fusty, musty moth-eaten era of the Victorian gentleman scientist. There are walls lined with fossils and glass cases of taxidermied birds. Even the much-loved **Diplodocus dinosaur skeleton** in the entrance hall and the huge, but tired-looking, **blue whale** are undeniably old-school attractions. The museum's animatronic dinosaurs,

including the 4m-high tyrannosaurus rex, will be on European tour for the next few years, but smaller animatronic raptors are still in the dinosaur exhibition.

Entering the Earth Galleries, by contrast, you'll wonder whether you've stumbled into a ritzy Italian nightclub, as displays of crystals, gems and precious rocks line its black walls. Four life-size human

INFORMATION

- ☎ 7942 5000
- 🖳 www.nhm.ac.uk
- ✉ Cromwell Rd SW7
- £ free
- 🕙 10am-5.50pm Mon-Sat, 11am-5.50pm Sun
- ℹ book for free Darwin Centre tours online (75p booking fee) or at the information desk (free)
- ⊖ South Kensington
- ♿ excellent
- 🍴 Globe Café, Life Galleries Restaurant, Waterhouse Cafe, Picnic Area

DON'T MISS

- · Blue whale exhibit
- · Stuffed dodo
- · Diplodocus dinosaur skeleton
- · Creepy crawlies
- · Animatronic dinosaurs
- · Ecology Gallery's Quadrascope video wall
- · Minerals and gems in the Earth Galleries

The museum's fabulously ornate façade

statues line the path to the escalator, which then slithers up through a hollowed-out globe into displays about our planet's geological make-up. **Volcanoes**, **earthquakes** and **storms** are all discussed here. However, the supposed star attraction, a mock-up of a small Japanese grocery shop that trembles in a manner meant to replicate the 1995 Kobe earthquake, is disappointingly lame. Other sections explore how planets form and the earth's ecology.

VICTORIA & ALBERT MUSEUM   (2, C5)

It boasts it's the world's greatest museum of applied art and design, but since Prince Albert (Queen Victoria's husband) bequeathed it to the nation after the Great Exhibition in 1851, the V&A doesn't seem to have observed *any* curatorial limits. With nearly four million displayed pieces, from Islamic art to Bauhaus chairs, via silver, porcelain and fake plaster statues, it's a bit like the nation's attic. So before you rummage around in this magnificent jumble it pays to know what you're looking for.

Many make a beeline past the huge, blue-green extruded **glass chandelier** by Dale Chihuly in the Cromwell Rd entrance to Room 40 on the same level (Level 1), where they find **costumes** and **fashion** ranging from absurd 18th-century wigs to the platform shoes that brought Naomi Campbell crashing to the Paris catwalk. Other visitors head to the nearby collection of Raphael's cartoons, or sketches (Room 48A). The **Green Dining Room** by the father of the Arts and Crafts movement, William Morris, is also found on Level 1, behind the relaxing Pirelli Garden.

The V&A – a decorative art lover's delight

The relatively new **British Galleries**, on Levels 2 and 4, chronicle British design from 1500 to 1900, while the **20th-century design galleries** on Level 3 house objects such as chairs by Ron Arad and a Dyson vacuum cleaner.

The largest collection of Constables under one roof are found in the **Henry Cole Wing**, on the Exhibition Rd side, but perhaps the museum's strongest point is its headline-grabbing **temporary exhibitions**. So don't forget to check current listings.

INFORMATION

☎ 7942 2000
🖥 www.vam.ac.uk
✉ Cromwell Rd SW7
£ free, donation of £3 requested
🕑 10am-5.45pm Mon-Sun, to 10pm Wed & last Fri of month
ℹ free 1hr tours 10.30am-3.30pm (plus Wed 4.30pm)
⊖ South Kensington
♿ excellent
🍴 The New Restaurant at the V&A

Spiral of Controversy

Over the next decade, the V&A galleries are being reshaped, so that the museum will resemble a city with a series of quarters, including Europe (with the new British Galleries), Asia, Contemporary Design and more. The most controversial, and talked-about, proposed change has been the so-called Spiral extension, designed by Daniel Libeskind. The twisted geometry of the postmodern extension enraged locals, before winning the backing of the English Heritage organisation. Financial constraints mean the £75 million project has been delayed until 2008. Meanwhile, Libeskind has been busying himself with the new building at New York's Ground Zero.

SCIENCE MUSEUM (2, C5)

Apart from items of historical import, such as the Apollo 10 command module and Stephenson's Rocket steam-engine train, it's the high-tech **Wellcome Wing** that wins the popular vote here. Not only are the whizz-bang **SimEx Simulator Ride** and **IMAX cinema** found within its confines, but it also keeps the young (and young at heart) entertained with visions of the future. There's a superlative exploration of identity on Level 1 entitled **Who am I?** and **hands-on displays** for children in the basement.

Back in the main building, you'll find yourself entering a large hall with a red mill engine from the early 20th century, before proceeding towards a history of the Industrial Revolution. Here on the ground floor there's also a **space exhibition**, which looks as creaky and outdated as the space shuttle – but still attracts awed devotees.

On the upper floors are displays on time and food (Level 1), then maths and computing (Level 2), where you'll find a re-creation of Charles Babbage's **mechanical calculator** (1832), the famous forerunner to the computer. The 3rd floor is another favourite place for children, with its gliders, hot-air balloon and varied aircraft; it also features an adapted flight simulator that's been turned into a **Motionride** (£2.50/1.50).

The museum's 4th and 5th floors contain exhibits on medical and veterinary history. By this stage, however, most parents will have been pestered back downstairs for a stopover in the huge ground-floor **shop**.

INFORMATION

- ☎ 0870 870 4868
- 🖳 www.sciencemu seum.org.uk
- ✉ Exhibition Rd SW7
- £ museum free; IMAX cinema £7.50/6; SimEx ride £3.75/ 2.75
- 🕑 10am-6pm (museum & IMAX cinema)
- ⊖ South Kensington
- ♿ excellent
- ✗ Deep Blue Café

DON'T MISS

- Apollo 10 command module
- Boulton & Watt's steam engine
- Venture Motionride flight simulator
- Wells cathedral clock (1392)
- Amy Johnson's *Gipsy Moth*

Everything you ever wanted to know about rocket science and more

CHARLOTTE HINDLE

ROYAL OBSERVATORY (5, B3)

Stand with one foot in the world's western hemisphere and the other in the east, and then learn how the **Prime Meridian** of longitude you've just strad-dled came to be located here: these are the two obvious things to do at the Royal Observatory in Greenwich. However, beware that the second involves a relatively complicated – albeit entrancing – story.

The building dates from 1675, when ships regularly ran aground because they were unable to meas-ure their east–west coordinates, or longitude. King Charles II ordered its construction in the belief that astronomy could resolve this navigational problem, and astron-omers royal from John Flamsteed onwards set up home here to work on the solution. Their living quar-ters and the **Octagon Room** from which they charted the heavens still survive, the latter being a rare example of interior design by Sir Christopher Wren.

Ultimately, the navigational an-swer proved not to be in the stars; Yorkshireman John Harrison solved the obdurate longitude problem with a well-crafted timepiece (see the boxed text). However, Green-wich was still named the Prime Me-ridian in 1884, in recognition of its

INFORMATION
- ☎ 8312 6565
- 🖳 www.nmm.ac.uk
- ✉ Greenwich Park SE10
- £ observatory free; planetarium £4/2
- 🕙 observatory 10am-6pm Apr-Sep, 10am-5pm Oct-Mar; planetarium 2.30pm Mon-Fri, 1.30pm & 3.30pm Sat, 2pm & 3pm Sun
- 🚊 DLR Cutty Sark
- ♿ good
- ✕ Trafalgar Tavern (p83)

The Longitude Solution

Medieval sailors calculated their north–south position, or latitude, using a sextant to measure the height of the sun or the Pole Star on the horizon. But even by the 17th century ships still couldn't work out longitude. Scientists knew one answer might lie in comparing local time (measured by the sun) with the time at one's home port. (If it takes 24 hours for the earth to turn 360°, a one-hour difference represents 15° longitude.) John Har-rison was the first to make a clock reliable enough, even while aboard a pitching ship, to keep an accurate record of home time.

Meridian Building, Royal Observatory

work, and GMT (Greenwich Mean Time) began to act as standard time worldwide. Today, the observatory has also embraced Harrison's ef-forts, displaying his original watch or **marine chronometer** (H4) and the three clocks (H1 to H3) that preceded it.

SAATCHI GALLERY   (3, E5)

Many of the greatest hits of Young British Art (YBA) are found in the Saatchi Gallery at County Hall, from Damien Hirst's **pickled sheep**, **shark** and **cows** to Tracey Emin's *My Bed* (littered and unmade). We can only say 'many of', because of two incidents that occurred after adman Charles Saatchi moved his collection to this grandiloquent Edwardian building in 2003. Firstly, an alleged spat saw Hirst reportedly buying back some of his works, and then a warehouse fire in 2004 destroyed some iconic works that had been in storage.

INFORMATION

☎ 7823 2363
🖥 www.saatchi-gallery.co.uk
✉ County Hall, Westminster Bridge Rd SE1
£ £8.75/6.75
🕐 10am-6pm, to 10pm Fri & Sat
⊖ Westminster/ Waterloo
✗ People's Palace in Royal Festival Hall (p75)

Discover the art behind the adman

Still, Saatchi undeniably has the ability to pick the works that define an era. More than sufficient pieces remain to chart the YBA movement from its beginnings in 1992 to its peak in the late 1990s. These include Ron Mueck's small but eerily lifelike *Dead Dad* sculpture; Chris Ofili's *The Holy Virgin Mary* (paint, paper, glitter and elephant dung); Marcus Harvey's huge *Myra* (the face of Moors child-murderer Myra Hindley, made up of thousands of stencilled child handprints); and Sarah Lucas' *Au Naturel* (two melons and a bucket, plus two oranges and a cucumber, arranged like a naked couple on a mattress).

Other highlights are works by Gavin Turk, Jake and Dinos Chapman and Richard Wilson's *20:50*, an overwhelming **oil-filled room**, whose smell permeates the gallery.

With one movement now safely under his belt, Saatchi seems ready to start defining a new era. Since 2004 particularly, he's been collecting new German and other Continental art.

The YBA Movement

Although most of this movement's major players are now in their 40s, the moniker Young British Art has stuck. It had its genesis in a group of Hoxton-based creatives producing cheeky, conceptual pieces often bought by high-profile collectors such as Jay Jopling (see the White Cube, p33) and Saatchi. Having peaked when the Royal Academy (see p33) staged the huge *Sensation* exhibition of pickled cows, anatomically incorrect mannequins and similar in 1997, the movement has been declared dead several times since. But, both controversial and populist, its works retain appeal for the viewing public, if not the critics.

SOMERSET HOUSE (6, F3)

Fifty-five fountains dancing in summer in its courtyard, which in winter is transformed into a popular ice rink, have helped to make this magnificent former tax office another millennial hit.

In fact, the Inland Revenue still occupies two of this Palladian building's wings, but the chief permanent attraction for non-accountant types is the newer **Courtauld Gallery** near the Strand entrance. Only a portion of the marvellous five-part permanent collection is on display at any one time, but it includes works by Botticelli, Bruegel, Cranach, Rubens, and Bloomsbury artists such as Vanessa Bell, Roger Fry and Duncan Grant. The centrepiece is the impressionist and postimpressionist collection,

INFORMATION

- ☎ 7845 4600
- 🖵 www.somerset-house.org.uk
- ✉ The Strand WC2
- £ for 1/2/3 collections £5/8/12, £1 discount for seniors & students, Courtauld Gallery free 10am-2pm Mon
- 🕑 10am-6pm
- ⓘ Various tours and audioguides available
- ⊖ Embankment/ Temple (closed Sun)
- ♿ excellent
- 🍴 Coffee Gallery, the Admiralty restaurant

DON'T MISS

- Botticelli's *The Trinity*
- Manet's *Le Déjeuner sur l'Herbe*
- Modigliani's *Nude*
- Renoir's *La Loge*
- Van Gogh's *Self-Portrait with Bandaged Ear*

which includes paintings and sculptures by Cézanne, Degas, Gauguin, Henri Rousseau, Manet, Monet, Sisley, Renoir, Toulouse-Lautrec and Van Gogh. Paintings by Russian émigrés Wassily Kandinsky and Alexej Jawlensksy are also due to remain on loan to the gallery for some time.

Somerset House (1775) is home to two other notable collections. The Courtauld Institute now runs the exhibitions in the **Hermitage Rooms** in conjunction with the State Hermitage Museum in St Petersburg. Ornate silver and Florentine mosaic cabinets are found in the **Gilbert Collection** at the Victoria Embankment entrance.

Get a fine-art fix at Somerset House

Sights & Activities

MUSEUMS

From major attractions such as the superlative National Maritime Museum and Imperial War Museum to smaller, quirkier exhibitions, London caters to every taste.

Cabinet War Rooms (3, D5)

'We will fight them on the beaches', Winston Churchill famously told the nation in a broadcast from this tomb-like bunker, where his government took refuge during WWII. From 2005, a new Churchill Museum will join the perfectly preserved Map Room and reconstructed bedrooms.

☎ 7930 6961
🖳 www.iwm.org.uk
✉ Clive Steps, King Charles St SW1
£ £7/5.50, children free
🕑 9.30am-6pm May-Sep, 10am-6pm Oct-Apr
⊖ Westminster/St James's Park 🚻 excellent

Dali Universe (3, E5)

This gallery's black walls, low lighting and mirrors make it seem like the surrealist artist's deliciously twisted subconscious. On display are melted watches, fire, crutches, a lobster telephone, a Mae West lips sofa and more.

☎ 7620 2720
🖳 www.daliuniverse.com
✉ County Hall, Westminster Bridge Rd SE1, entrance on Albert Embankment
£ £8.50/5-7.50, family £24 🕑 10am-5.30pm
⊖ Westminster/Waterloo

Design Museum (3, J5)

This sparkling white building is the place to enthuse over the latest objects of modern design, before snaffling yourself a slice of aesthetic perfection in the shop. Recent exhibitions have featured Manolo Blahnik's shoes and avant-garde architecture of the '60s.

☎ 7940 8790 🖳 www.designmuseum.org
✉ 28 Shad Thames SE1
£ £6/4, family £16
🕑 10am-5.45pm
⊖ Tower Hill/London Bridge 🚻 good

Fashion & Textile Museum (3, J5)

In the world capital of street style, what better than to catch up on the changing exhibitions of contemporary designer frocks, textiles and catwalk accessories in this cool Mediterranean building?

☎ 7403 0222 🖳 www.ftmlondon.org ✉ 83 Bermondsey St SE1 £ £6/4 🕑 10am-4.45pm Tue-Sun ⊖ London Bridge 🚻 excellent

Geffrye Museum (2, H2)

With a sequence of re-created domestic interiors along 14 interconnected almshouses, running chronologically from Elizabethan times to the end of the 20th century, this museum is a lot more edifying than any ordinary furniture showroom.

☎ 7739 9893 🖳 www.geffrye-museum.org.uk
✉ 136 Kingsland Rd E2
£ free, donations appreciated 🕑 10am-5pm Tue-Sat, noon-5pm Sun ⊖ London Bridge then bus 243 or rail Dalston Kingsland 🚻 excellent

Imperial War Museum (3, F6)

Even committed pacifists appreciate the Imperial War Museum. That's because, alongside its internationally famous collection of planes, tanks and other military hardware, it provides a telling lesson in modern history. Highlights include a re-created WWI trench and bomb shelter and a Holocaust exhibition.

☎ 7416 5320/09001 600140 🖳 www.iwm.org.uk ✉ Lambeth Rd SE1 £ free 🕑 10am-6pm ⊖ Waterloo/Lambeth North 🚻 good

Kenwood House (2, D1)

Housing a small collection of paintings by Gainsborough, Reynolds, Rembrandt, Turner and Vermeer, this neoclassical mansion (1773) set in magnificent grounds beside Hampstead Heath is a perfect picture of Jane Austen Englishness.

☎ 8348 1286 🖳 www.english-heritage.org.uk
✉ Hampstead La NW3
£ free 🕑 house 10am-5pm Apr-Oct, 10am-4pm Nov-Mar; grounds 8am-sunset ⊖ Archway/Golders Green, then bus 210 🚻 good

London's Transport Museum (6, F2)

Learn how London made the transition from horse-drawn carriages to the tube, the Docklands Light Rail (DLR) and the ultramodern Jubilee line extension.

☎ 7379 6344 or 7565 7299 (recorded information) 🖳 www.ltmuseum.co.uk ✉ Covent Garden Piazza WC2 £ £5.95/2.50-4.50 ◷ 10am-6pm Sat-Thu, 11am-6pm Fri ↔ Covent Garden ♿ good

MCC Museum & Lord's Tour (2, C2)

The Ashes trophy never leaves this famous cricket ground, much to the chagrin of winning Australian teams. But the club *has* broken with tradition by erecting a media centre resembling a spaceship.

☎ 7432 1033 🖳 www.lords.org ✉ Marylebone Cricket Club NW8 £ £7/5.50 ◷ tours noon & 2pm, plus 10am Apr-Sep ↔ St John's Wood

Museum in Docklands (p45)

Trying to paint a general Thames history, this place fares best when focusing on its own river bend, ie the controversial conversion of the neglected docks neighbourhoods into a financial hub during the 1980s.

☎ 7515 1162 🖳 www.museumindocklands.org.uk ✉ No 1 Warehouse, West India Quay E14 £ £5/3, children free ◷ 10am-5.30pm

↔ Canary Wharf or 🚃 DLR West India Quay ♿ good

Museum of London (3, G3)

Savvy Londoners list this place as a favourite. More than one million objects, ranging from the ice age to the Internet – including re-created Roman streets, a gilded coach and a Great Fire diorama – lay out the rich tapestry of the city's history.

☎ 7600 0807 🖳 www.museumoflondon.org.uk ✉ London Wall EC2 £ free ◷ 10am-5.50pm Mon-Sat, noon-5.50pm Sun ↔ Barbican ♿ excellent

National Maritime Museum (5, B2)

Inigo Jones' magnificent neoclassical building hosts an impressive collection that even confirmed landlubbers shouldn't miss. The glass-roofed Neptune Court, a golden 18th-century royal barge, the *Passengers* cruise liners exhibit and the uniform Nelson was wearing when fatally shot are just several of many highlights.

☎ 8312 6565 🖳 www.nmm.ac.uk ✉ Romney Rd SE10 £ free, prices vary for temporary exhibitions ◷ 10am-6pm Apr-Sep, 10am-5pm Oct-Mar 🚃 DLR Cutty Sark ♿ good

Sherlock Holmes Museum (3, A2)

Like its address – which should be 239 (where the fictional Holmes lived)

instead of the advertised 221b – this homage to Sir Arthur Conan Doyle's fictional detective slightly misses the mark. Waxworks and mementos 'left' by Watson and Holmes are rather tacky, but die-hard fans will still enjoy.

☎ 7935 8866 🖳 www.sherlock-holmes.co.uk ✉ 221b Baker St NW1 £ £6/4 ◷ 9.30am-6pm ↔ Baker St

Sir John Soane's Museum (6, F1)

Architect Soane (1753–1837) crammed his home with statues, Hogarth paintings (including the original *Rake's Progress*), an Egyptian sarcophagus, an imitation monk's parlour and other *objets d'art*. It's still as he left it, in one of London's most satisfyingly quirky museums.

☎ 7405 2107 🖳 www.soane.org ✉ 13 Lincoln's Inn Fields WC2 £ free, tours £3 ◷ 10am-5pm Tue-Sat, plus 6-9pm 1st Tue of month, tours 2.30pm Sat ↔ Holborn

Theatre Museum (6, F2)

This branch of the Victoria & Albert Museum features a vast array of costumes and artefacts relating to the history of the theatre, opera and ballet, as well as memorabilia from great thespians.

☎ 7943 4700 🖳 www.theatremuseum.org ✉ 7 Russell St WC2 £ free ◷ 10am-6pm Tue-Sun ↔ Covent Garden ♿ excellent

GALLERIES

London is home to some of the world's most exciting galleries. While the Wallace Collection and Dulwich Picture Gallery offer permanent fine-art collections, the other venues listed rely on spectacular temporary exhibitions throughout the year.

Dulwich Picture Gallery (1, C2)

Part art gallery – the UK's oldest – and part tomb, this neoclassical building (1814) was designed by Sir John Soane. Even in death, founders Noel Desenfans and Francis Bourgeois couldn't bear to leave their Rembrandts, Rubens, Reynolds and Gainsboroughs, and both are buried here. The new annexe (2000) hosts temporary exhibits.
☎ 8693 5254 🖳 www.dulwichpicturegallery.org.uk ✉ Gallery Rd SE21 £ £4/3, plus £3 for special exhibitions ⏲ 10am-5pm Tue-Fri, 11am-5pm Sat & Sun 🚈 West Dulwich ♿ good

Hayward Gallery (3, E5)

New foyer notwithstanding, the trick with the monolithic Hayward is to get inside quick – away from the ugly concrete exterior into the roomy, modernist interiors that provide a perfect backdrop to the leading international exhibitions of contemporary and experimental art held here.
☎ 0870 382 8000 (tickets) or 7921 0930 (information) 🖳 www.sbc.org.uk ✉ Belvedere Rd SW1 £ prices vary ⏲ times vary: usually 10am-6pm Mon-Sun, to 8pm Tue-Wed, to 9pm Fri ⊖ Waterloo ♿ good

Institute of Contemporary Arts (3, C5)

Being housed in a wedding-cake–style Regency terrace only makes this modern art gallery even cooler – sneak a peek at the magnificent Nash Room upstairs if you can. Otherwise, there are rotating exhibitions of painting, photography, video, installation art and architecture. Head for the ICA's equally cool café if you need a break.
☎ 7930 3647 🖳 www.ica.org.uk ✉ The Mall SW1 £ prices vary ⏲ noon-7.30pm ⊖ Charing Cross/Piccadilly Circus ♿ fair

Photographers' Gallery (6, D2)

So small that it uses the walls of its neighbouring

Fire-breathing sculpture, Royal Academy of Arts forecourt

café as additional exhibition space, this modern gallery punches well above its weight in influence. Past winners of its annual Citigroup Photography Prize (held from January to March) include Richard Billingham, Andreas Gursky, Boris Mikhailov and Juergen Teller.
☎ 7831 1772
🖥 www.photonet.org.uk
✉ 5 & 8 Great Newport St WC2 £ free
🕑 11am-6pm Mon-Sat, noon-6pm Sun
⊖ Leicester Sq/Charing Cross ♿ good

Royal Academy of Arts (6, B3)

Major plans are underway to expand this already monumental fine-arts institution. The Summer Exhibition, open to all entrants and held between early June and mid-August, is hugely popular.
☎ 7300 8000 or 7300 5760 (recorded information) 🖥 www .royalacademy.org.uk
✉ Burlington House, Piccadilly W1 £ prices vary 🕑 10am-6pm Mon-Sun, to 10pm Fri
⊖ Green Park
♿ excellent

Serpentine Gallery (2, C4)

The simple, open-plan layout of this Hyde Park former teahouse make it excellent for installation art, as well as paintings and photography. Watch for the temporary Summer Pavilion, designed by a different celebrity architect each year.
☎ 7402 6075 🖥 www .serpentinegallery.org
✉ Kensington Gardens

What's On?
For information on the ever-changing exhibitions in London's commercial galleries, check out **New Exhibitions of Contemporary Art** (www.new exhibitions.com).

(near Albert Memorial)
£ free 🕑 10am-6pm
⊖ South Kensington/ Knightsbridge
♿ excellent

Wallace Collection (3, A3)

This treasure-trove of paintings from the 17th and 18th centuries is almost criminally neglected by Londoners and tourists alike. Inside its splendid Italianate mansion, you'll find works by Rubens, Titian, Poussin, Frans Hals and Rembrandt.
☎ 7563 9500 🖥 www .wallacecollection.org
✉ Hertford House, Manchester Sq W1
£ free 🕑 10am-5pm Mon-Sat, noon-5pm Sun
⊖ Bond St
♿ excellent

Whitechapel Art Gallery (2, H3)

Behind an Art Nouveau interior lies the gallery responsible for first bringing Frida Kahlo and Nan Goldin to fame in England. It still manages to challenge, with shows on leading architects, talks by Hollywood directors and eye-catching art works. A £10 million expansion, due to open by 2007, will mean even more dynamic exhibitions.
☎ 7522 7888 🖥 www .whitechapel.org
✉ 80-82 Whitechapel High St E1 £ prices vary 🕑 11am-6pm Tue-Sun, to 9pm Thu ⊖ Aldgate East ♿ excellent

White Cube (3, J1)

With the Saatchi Gallery (p28) now part of the mainstream, Jay Jopling's trendy Hoxton gallery is the new flag-bearer for cutting-edge Britart. It's the place to go looking for the next Tracey Emin or Damien Hirst.
☎ 7930 5373 🖥 www .whitecube.com ✉ 48 Hoxton Sq N1 £ free
🕑 10am-6pm Tue-Sat
⊖ Old St ♿ fair

The East End's innovative Whitechapel Art Gallery

SIMON BRACKEN

NOTABLE BUILDINGS & MONUMENTS

Some highlights on the skyline, such as the gherkin-shaped Swiss Re Tower (3, J3) and the Millennium Dome (1, C1) in North Greenwich, can only be admired from afar. Those below offer a closer view.

Albert Memorial (2, C4)
As over-the-top as Queen Victoria's love for her German husband, Albert, this neo-Gothic monument (1872) by architect Sir George Gilbert Scott gleams after major renovations in the late 1990s.
☎ 7495 0916 ✉ Hyde Park, Kensington Gore SW7 £ tours £3.50/3 ⏰ tours 2pm & 3pm Sun ⊖ South Kensington ♿ good

British Library (3, D1)
Colin St John's new British Library (1998) has copped some flak for its red-brick façade, but the interior is superb. Only members can use the famous collection, but historical documents, including the Magna Carta, are on public display.
☎ 7412 7000/7332 🖳 www.bl.uk ✉ 96 Euston Rd NW1 £ free ⏰ 9.30am-6pm Mon-Fri, to 8pm Tue, 9.30am-5pm Sat, 11am-5pm Sun ⊖ King's Cross St Pancras ♿ excellent

City Hall (3, J5)
London's answer to Berlin's *Reichstag* (Parliament), the City Hall (aka the 'testicle') is regularly open to the public.
☎ 7983 4100 🖳 www .london.gov.uk ✉ The Queen's Walk SE1 £ free ⏰ usually two weekends per month (check website), café 9am-5pm ⊖ Tower Hill/London Bridge ♿ excellent

The Monument (3, H4)
Topped with a gilded bronze urn of flames, this 60m stone column was designed by Sir Christopher Wren to commemorate the Great Fire, which began in a nearby bakery in 1666. Tight steps (311 of them) lead to a balcony offering panoramic views over the City.
☎ 7626 2717 ✉ Monument St EC3 £ £2/1 ⏰ 9.30am-5pm ⊖ Monument

Old Royal Naval College (5, B2)
This Wren masterpiece is now home to the University of Greenwich, but you can still view the mural-covered Painted Hall in the King William Building and the fabulous Chapel in the Queen Mary Building, opposite.
☎ 8269 4747, 0800 389 3341 ✉ King William Walk SE10 £ free ⏰ 10am-5pm Mon-Sat, 12.30-5pm Sun 🚉 DLR Cutty Sark

Thames Flood Barrier (1, C1)
More than 25 years old, this line of sail-like floodgates still looks futuristically surreal, like a Martian-style Sydney Opera House. The 11 gates look best when raised, so ring to find out when they'll next be tested.
☎ 8305 4188 🖳 www.environment-agency.co.uk ✉ 1 Unity Way SE18 £ barrier free, information centre £1/50-75p ⏰ 10.30am-4.30pm Apr-Sep, 11am-3.30pm Oct-Nov ⊖ North Greenwich, or rail Charlton & then bus 161, 177, 180 🚢 to/from Greenwich Pier (☎ 7930 4097; www .westminsterpier.co.uk)

Tower Bridge (3, J5)
Globally recognised as a symbol of London, this Victorian bridge takes visitors up into its 25m-high twin towers via lifts (elevators). The raised walkways also afford excellent views.
☎ 7940 3985 🖳 www .towerbridge.org.uk ✉ Tower Bridge SE1 £ £4.50/3, family £19.50 ⏰ 10am-6pm Apr-Oct, from 10.30am Nov-Mar ⊖ Tower Hill ♿ good

Wellington Arch (3, B5)
Built in 1826 to commemorate Wellington's victories over Napoleon, the arch has three floors of exhibition space and a viewing platform with spectacular vistas of the park and Houses of Parliament.
☎ 7930 2726 🖳 www .english-heritage.org.uk ✉ Hyde Park Cnr W1 £ £3/1.80-2.50; joint ticket with Wellington Museum (see p38) £6/3-5, family £15 ⏰ 10am-5pm Wed-Sun Apr-Oct, to 4pm Wed-Sun Nov-Mar ⊖ Hyde Park Corner ♿ good

CHURCHES & CATHEDRALS

St Bartholomew-the-Great (3, G3)

One of London's oldest churches and arguably its most atmospheric, St Bartholomew-the-Great featured in *Four Weddings and a Funeral*. Norman arches encase a dimly lit interior.

☎ 7606 5171
🖳 www.greatstbarts.com
✉ West Smithfield EC1
🕑 8.30am-5pm Tue-Fri, 10.30am-1.30pm Sat, 8am-8pm Sun
⊖ Barbican/Farringdon
♿ good

St Bride's (3, F3)

St Bride's (designed by Wren in 1671) is still called the journalists' church, although the newspaper industry has long left Fleet St. Beneath the famous wedding-cake steeple, plaques honour journalists killed in the line of duty.

☎ 7427 0133 ✉ Fleet St EC4 🕑 8am-4.45pm Mon-Fri, 10am-3pm Sat ⊖ St Paul's or 🚉 Blackfriars/City Thameslink ♿ fair

St Martin-in-the-Fields (6, D3)

An early 18th-century masterpiece by James Gibbs, this celebrated church occupies a prime site on Trafalgar Square and helps form one of London's greatest vistas. Its tradition of tending to the poor and homeless goes back to WWI.

☎ 7766 1109 🖳 www.stmartin-in-the-fields.org
✉ Trafalgar Sq WC2
🕑 8am-6.30pm
⊖ Charing Cross

St Mary-le-Bow (3, G3)

This is the famous church (Wren, 1673) whose bells dictate who is – and who isn't – a cockney; if you were born within the sound of their peal, you're the genuine article. The delicate steeple is particularly impressive.

☎ 7248 5139 🖳 www.stmarylebow.co.uk
✉ Cheapside EC2
🕑 6.30am-6pm Mon-Thu, 6.30am-4pm Fri
⊖ Bank/St Paul's

St Stephen Wallbrook (3, H4)

A small forerunner to St Paul's Cathedral, this light, airy building (1679) has 16 Corinthian pillars supporting its ceiling and dome. In the middle of the floor is a round altar, sculpted by Henry Moore, that's dubbed the 'camembert' because of its shape.

☎ 7283 4444
✉ 39 Walbrook EC3
🕑 10am-4pm Mon-Thu, 10am-3pm Fri ⊖ Bank
♿ good

Southwark Cathedral (3, H4)

The oft-overlooked 'Cinderella of London cathedrals' is a mishmash of medieval and Victorian styles. There's a memorial to Shakespeare, plus a new multimedia exhibition examining Southwark and surrounds during the past 2000 years.

☎ 7367 6700
🖳 www.dswark.org
✉ Montague Close SE1

£ cathedral free, £4 donation requested; exhibition £3/1-2.50
🕑 8am-6pm, evensong 5.30pm Mon-Fri, 4pm Sat, 3pm Sun ⊖ London Bridge ♿ good

Temple Church (3, F3)

The only church with a round interior in London, this was built by the secretive Knights Templar in 1185. Its frequently shifting opening times are just as mysterious as its founders, so ring ahead.

☎ 7353 8559 🖳 www.templechurch.com
✉ King's Bench Walk, Inner Temple EC4
🕑 11am-6pm Wed-Fri, 11am-2.30pm Sat, 12.45-2.45pm Sun
⊖ Temple/Blackfriars
♿ good

Westminster Cathedral (3, C6)

The British headquarters of the Roman Catholic church is the only good example of neo-Byzantine architecture in London. The views from the distinctive candy-striped red-brick and white-stone tower are phenomenal.

☎ 7798 9055
🖳 www.westminstercathedral.org.uk
✉ Victoria St SW1
£ cathedral free; tower £2/1, family £5
🕑 cathedral 7am-7pm Mon-Fri, 7am-8pm Sat & Sun; tower 9.30am-5pm Apr-Sep, 9.30am-5pm Thu-Sun Nov-Mar
⊖ Victoria ♿ good (cathedral only)

PARKS & GARDENS

Battersea Park (2, D6)
A Japanese Peace Pagoda, a children's zoo and rowing boats for hire (£4.60) are all reasons to visit this 50-hectare stretch of greenery and lakes between Albert and Chelsea Bridges.
☎ 8871 7534
✉ Albert Bridge Rd SW11 🕐 dawn-dusk 🚇 Battersea Park/Queenstown Rd (Battersea) ♿ excellent

Chelsea Physic Garden (2, D6)
Created in 1673 by the Apothecaries' Society livery company to study the relationship of botany to medicine (then known as the physic art), this peaceful oasis is one of Europe's oldest botanical gardens.
☎ 7352 5646
💻 www.chelseaphysic garden.co.uk ✉ 66

Royal Hospital Rd SW3 (entrance on Swan Walk) 💷 £5/3 🕐 noon-5pm Wed Apr-Oct, 2-6pm Sun (noon-5pm Mon-Fri during Chelsea Flower Show in May) 🚇 Sloane Sq ♿ excellent

Greenwich Park (5, B3)
Partly the work of Le Nôtre, who landscaped Versailles, this park contains a grand avenue, a lovely rose garden and the Royal Observatory (see p27), among other things.

It slopes up a hill, where you have great views of the Inigo Jones buildings below and, across the river, Canary Wharf.
☎ 8858 2608
✉ King William Walk SE10 🕐 7am-dusk 🚇 DLR Cutty Sark ♿ good

Hampstead Heath (2, D1)
Bathing ponds, picnic spots and playing fields dot these partly wild and unmanicured 320 hectares. Kenwood House (see p30)

London's Wildlife
Alongside the Wetland Centre, London has more than 50 nature reserves maintained by the **London Wildlife Trust** (☎ 7261 0447; www.wildlondon .org.uk). Battersea Park Nature Reserve has several nature trails, while parts of Hampstead Heath are designated Sites of Special Scientific Interest (SSSIs) for their wealth of natural history.

Free range, free speech – free food? No… Free strolls, Regent's Park

is also found here. However, the high point is Parliament Hill, which offers unparalleled views of the London skyline and is a popular place to fly a kite.
☎ 7485 4491
✉ Hampstead Heath NW3 ☽ 24hr
⊖ Hampstead or
🚊 Gospel Oak/Hampstead Heath
♿ excellent

Hyde Park (2, C4)

This 145-hectare park is central London's largest. Under Henry VIII, it became a hunting ground for kings and aristocrats, and later a venue for duels, executions, horse racing and the site of the 1851 Great Exhibition. It's full of sunbathers and boats on the Serpentine in summer. On Park Lane, you'll see the intricately sculpted Queen Elizabeth Gate.
☎ 7298 2100
✉ Hyde Park W2
☽ 5.30am-midnight
⊖ Hyde Park Corner/Knightsbridge/Lancaster Gate/Marble Arch
♿ excellent

Regent's Park (3, A1)

Like many London parks, this was first used as a royal hunting ground, subsequently farmed and then revived as a place for leisure during the 18th century. It contains London Zoo (p41), the Grand Union Canal and an open-air theatre.
☎ 7486 7905
✉ Regent's Park NW1
☽ dawn-dusk
⊖ Baker St/Regent's Park ♿ excellent

Speak Your Mind

Every Sunday at **Speaker's Corner** (3, A4), just south of Marble Arch in Hyde Park, anyone with a soapbox can hold forth on any subject that takes their fancy. Get whatever is bugging you off your chest – the eccentrics and fanatics do.

Richmond Park (1, C1)

One of London's largest (1000 hectares) and wildest open spaces, Richmond Park is home to foxes, badgers, deer and other wildlife. It's a great place for bird-watchers too.
☎ 8948 3209
✉ Richmond, Surrey
☽ 7am-dusk Mar-Sep, 7.30am-dusk Oct-Feb
🚊 Richmond
♿ excellent

St James's Park (3, C5)

The neatest and most regal of London's parks, St James's has great vistas of Westminster, Buckingham Palace and St James's Palace.
☎ 7930 1793 ✉ The Mall SW1 ☽ 5am-dusk
⊖ St James's Park/Charing Cross
♿ excellent

Wetland Centre (2, A6)

Europe's largest inland wetland project was created from four Victorian

Speaker's Corner, Hyde Park

reservoirs in 2000. It attracts 130 species of birds and 300 types of moths and butterflies.
☎ 8409 4400
🖳 www.wetlandcentre.org.uk ✉ Queen Elizabeth's Walk SW13
£ £6.75/4-5.50, family £17.50 ☽ 9.30am-6pm summer, 9.30am-5pm winter
⊖ Hammersmith, then bus 283 (Duck Bus)
♿ excellent

London in Flower

Lovers of exotic plants shouldn't miss Kew Gardens (p21) but London's parks boast a wide range of common, garden-variety trees, shrubs and flowers. Many locals also take pride in their private gardens, some of which are open to the public for a few days each year (generally May to September) through the **National Gardens Scheme** (☎ 01483-211535; www.ngs.org.uk).

FAMOUS ABODES

Carlyle's House (2, C6)
The great essayist Thomas Carlyle wrote his history of the French Revolution in this Queen Anne residence. ☎ 7352 7087 ✉ 24 Cheyne Row SW3 £ £3.80/1.80 ☼ Apr-early Nov, 11am-5pm Wed-Sun ⊖ Sloane Sq

Dickens' House (3, E2)
This is the only surviving London residence of the great Victorian novelist's many homes. In a two-year stint (1837–39) here, he wrote *The Pickwick Papers*, *Nicholas Nickleby* and *Oliver Twist*. ☎ 7405 2127 ☐ www .dickensmuseum.com ✉ 49 Doughty St WC1 £ £5/3-4, family £14 ☼ 10am-5pm Mon-Sat, 11am-5pm Sun ⊖ Russell Sq

Dr Johnson's House (3, F3)
This Georgian townhouse hardly crackles with the wit of the great lexicographer, who said 'When a man is tired of London, he is tired of life'. However, it is well preserved. ☎ 7353 3745 ☐ www .drjohnsonshouse.org ✉ 17 Gough Sq EC4 £ £4/1-3, family £9 ☼ 11am-5.30pm Mon-Sat May-Sep, 11am-5pm Mon-Sat Oct-Apr ⊖ Blackfriars

Eltham Palace (1, C1)
Henry VIII lived under the hammer-beam roof of the medieval hall, but the stunning sight here is the adjacent Art Deco home built by a member of the Courtauld clan in the 1930s. ☎ 8294 2548 ☐ www .english-heritage.org.uk ✉ Court Rd SE9 £ £7/ 3.50-5.30, family £17.50 ☼ 10am-5pm Wed-Fri & Sun Apr-Sep, 10am-4pm Wed-Fri & Sun Oct-Xmas & Feb-Mar, closed Jan 🚃 Eltham ♿ good

Freud Museum (2, C1)
Sigmund Freud spent the last 18 months of his life here after fleeing Nazi-occupied Vienna. The house contains the psychoanalyst's original couch, his books and his Greek and Asian artefacts. ☎ 7435 2002 ☐ www .freud.org.uk ✉ 20 Maresfield Gardens NW3 £ £5/2, children free ☼ noon-5pm Wed-Sun ⊖ Finchley Rd ♿ fair

Handel House Museum (3, B4)
The first museum to be devoted to a composer in London celebrates the life and times of Handel. He lived here from 1723 until his death 36 years later. ☎ 7495 1685 ☐ www .handelhouse.org ✉ 23-25 Brook St W1 £ £4.50/ 2-3.50 ☼ 10am-6pm Tue-Sat, to 8pm Thu, noon-6pm Sun ⊖ Bond St/Oxford Circus ♿ excellent

Keats House (2, C1)
Sitting under a plum tree in the garden inspired the romantic poets' golden boy to write his most celebrated poem, *Ode to a Nightingale*. Plans to restore the décor to what it was in Keats' day will mean a three-month closure in spring 2005, so ring ahead. ☎ 7435 2062 ☐ www .keatshouse.org.uk ✉ Wentworth Pl, Keats Grove NW3 £ £3/1.50, children free ☼ noon-4pm Tue-Sun Nov-late Mar, noon-5pm Tue-Sun late Mar-Oct; tours by appointment only 10am-noon ⊖ Hampstead or 🚃 Hampstead Heath

Wellington Museum (3, B5)
Home to the duke of Wellington from 1817 to 1852, striking 18th-century Apsley House overlooking Hyde Park Corner retains most of its furnishings and collections. ☎ 7499 5676 ☐ www .english-heritage.org.uk ✉ 149 Piccadilly W1 £ £4.50/2.30-3, joint ticket with Wellington Arch (p34) £6/3-5, family £15 ☼ 10am-6pm Tue-Sun Apr-Oct, 10am-5pm Tue-Sun Nov-Mar ⊖ Hyde Park Corner ♿ fair

Blue Plaques
The practice of placing blue plaques on the houses of distinguished Londoners began in 1866. The original criteria for the placing of a plaque were that the candidate must have been dead for at least 20 years, born more than 100 years before and be known to the 'well-informed passer-by'.

QUIRKY LONDON

Dennis Severs' House (3, J2)
The rooms of this restored 18th-century house are uniquely strewn with the everyday possessions of a family of Huguenot silk weavers, who can sometimes be 'heard', just out of reach. Monday night's candlelight tours are most atmospheric.
☎ 7247 4013 🖳 www.dennisseversshouse.co.uk ✉ 18 Folgate St E1 £ Sun/Mon/Mon night £8/5/12 🕑 noon-2pm 1st & 3rd Sun of the month, noon-2pm Mon following 1st & 3rd Sun of the month, Mon night (times vary) ⊖ Liverpool St

Greenwich Foot Tunnel (5, A2)
There's no need for a miracle to help you walk across the Thames. Just nip down the 88 to 100 steps near Greenwich Pier or at the northern Island Gardens end and traverse this Victorian pedestrian tunnel beneath the river.
✉ Greenwich Pier £ free 🕑 24hr, lifts 7am-7pm Mon-Sat, 10am-5.30pm Sun 🚆 DLR Cutty Sark/Island Gardens ♿ good

Highgate Cemetery (2, E1)
This Victorian Valhalla offers a different Marx & Spencer: Communist Karl (Marx) and philosopher Herbert (Spencer) are both buried in the eastern sector, alongside novelist George Eliot (aka Mary Anne Evans), scientist Michael Faraday and others. The vine-covered western sector is by tour only; phone for details.
☎ 8340 1834 ✉ Swain's La N6 £ £2/1, tours £3/1 🕑 10am-5pm Mon-Fri, 11am-5pm Sat & Sun Apr-Oct, 10am-4pm Mon-Fri, 11am-4pm Sat & Sun Nov-Mar ⊖ Highgate ♿ good

Jubilee Line Extension (3, D5)
It might seem crazy to treat any part of London's miserably decrepit Underground rail system as an attraction. However, the newer Jubilee line stations east of Westminster – particularly Southwark, Canary Wharf and North Greenwich – just prove what wonders more investment can bring.
🕑 5.30am-midnight ⊖ Westminster

London Dungeon (3, H5)
Fear! Terror! Panic! And that's just the reaction to the queues outside this schlocky, mega-popular house of horrors. Inside, ketchup-bespattered actors ham it up as they hang from the gallows, fall ill with plague and generally suffer all the crime, torture and disasters historical London offered.
☎ 7403 7221 or 09001 600066 (recorded information) 🖳 www.thedungeons.com ✉ 28-34 Tooley St SE1 £ £14.50/9.75-12.75 🕑 10am-6.30pm Apr-Sep, 10am-5.30pm Oct-Mar ⊖ London Bridge ♿ good

A Highgate headstone

Old Bailey (Central Criminal Court; 3, F3)
Watch (sometimes patchy) British justice at work inside the court that sent down Oscar Wilde, Jeffrey Archer and the Kray Twins. Tight security and no lockers mean visitors must arrive without cameras, mobile phones, large bags or food.
☎ 7248 3277 ✉ cnr Newgate & Old Bailey Sts £ free 🕑 10am-1pm & 2-5pm Mon-Fri ⊖ St Paul's

Old Operating Theatre & Herb Garret (3, H5)
The primitive surgical tools of the 19th century will leave you more terrified than at the London Dungeon – and praising the heavens for the advances of modern medicine. An adjacent garret exhibits therapeutic herbs.
☎ 7955 4791 🖳 www.thegarret.org.uk ✉ 9a St Thomas St SE1 £ £4/2.50-3, family £10 🕑 10.30am-5pm ⊖ London Bridge

LONDON FOR CHILDREN

On the information line for **Visit London** (☎ 09068 663344; per min 60p), you can key a separate option to hear details about London for children.

Bethnal Green Museum of Childhood (2, J2)
The playthings displayed here offer an unashamedly nostalgic view of childhood, with only a brief nod to the contemporary. Rocking horses, vintage dolls, zoetropes and Meccano will have little ones exclaiming, 'You mean there were toys before Xbox, Mum?'
☎ 8980 2415 💻 www .museumofchildhood.org .uk ✉ Cambridge Heath Rd E2 £ free, play areas £1.80 🕐 10am-5.50pm Sat-Thu ⊖ Bethnal Green ♿ good

Cutty Sark (5, A2)
Summer weekends are best for children aboard the moored tea clipper *Cutty Sark* when there are shanty singers and costumed storytellers. But the collection of colourful figureheads will keep kids happy year round.
☎ 8858 3445 ✉ Cutty Sark Gardens, King William Walk SE10 £ £3.95/2.95, family

Baby-sitting
Need a bit of a break from the ankle biters? Contact **Childminders** (3, A2 ☎ 7935 2049 day, 7935 3000 night, 7487 5040 recorded information; www .babysitter.co.uk; 6 Nottingham St W1).

£9.80 🕐 10am-5pm 🚇 DLR Cutty Sark

Golden Hinde (3, H4)
This replica 16th-century galleon is a big hit with little people, particularly as it was designed for a typically 5ft 4in tall medieval crew. Modelled on the tiny ship in which Francis Drake first circumnavigated the globe, it also hosts Elizabethan costume sleepovers (per person £33) and kid's theme parties.
☎ 7403 0123 or 0870 011 8700 (sleepovers & theme parties) 💻 www .goldenhinde.co.uk ✉ Cathedral St SE1 £ £2.75/2-2.35, family £8 🕐 9am-5.30pm ⊖ London Bridge

HMS Belfast (3, J4)
A large WWII cruiser, the HMS *Belfast* is another ship museum that entertains kids of all ages.
☎ 7940 6300 💻 www .iwm.org.uk/belfast ✉ Morgan's La, Tooley St SE1 £ £6/4.40, children free 🕐 10am-6pm Mar-Oct, 10am-5pm Nov-Feb ⊖ London Bridge

London Aquarium (3, E5)
In the darkened walkways between the vast tanks, it's sometimes hard to tell whether there are more children watching exotically coloured fish, or fish watching noisy children. The manta rays can even be patted and there's a terrapin tank.
☎ 7967 8000 💻 www .londonaquarium.co.uk ✉ County Hall, Westminster Bridge Rd SE1, entrance on Albert Embankment £ £8.75/5.25-6.50, family £25 🕐 10am-6pm ⊖ Westminster/ Waterloo

London IMAX Cinema (3, E5)
With a screen 26m wide and 10 storeys high, plus 485 seats, Europe's largest

Give the kids free rein in London's many parks

Playgrounds

These two playgrounds in central London are particularly renowned and well equipped:

- **Coram's Fields** (3, E2 ☎ 7837 6138; 93 Guilford St WC1 ☼ 9am-8pm summer, 9am-dusk winter ⊖ Russell Sq)
- **Diana, Princess of Wales Memorial Playground** (2, C4 ☎ 7928 2117 or 7928 2141 for recorded information; Black Lion Gate, Broad Walk, Kensington Gardens ☼ 10am-8pm summer, 10am-dusk winter ⊖ Queensway/Bayswater)

IMAX cinema hosts the usual documentaries about travel, wildlife and space. ☎ 7902 1234 ▢ www .bfi.org.uk/imax ✉ 1 Charlie Chaplin Walk SE1 £ £7.50/4.95-6.20, plus £1 advance booking fee, additional films £4.20 each ☼ 7 screenings 1-9pm daily, 2 extra screenings 10.30am & 11.45am Fri & Sat ⊖ Waterloo

London Trocadero (6, C3)

The noise levels almost register on the Richter scale in this indoor entertainment complex. Six levels of video games and high-tech rides are anchored by the Funland indoor theme park. ☎ 7292 3636 (Funland) ▢ www .londontrocadero.com ✉ Piccadilly Circus W1 £ per ride £2 ☼ 10am-midnight Sun-Thu, 10am-1am Fri & Sat ⊖ Piccadilly Circus Ƌ good

London Zoo (4, A3)

This zoo takes an educational angle in its popular Web of Life exhibition and its focus on conservation and breeding

has helped save some species from extinction. Its most famous inhabitants, however, remain the penguins strutting around architect Berthold Lubetkin's celebrated pool. ☎ 7722 3333 ▢ www .londonzoo.co.uk ✉ Regent's Park NW1 £ £13/9.75-11, family £41 ☼ 10am-5.30pm Mar-Oct, 10am-4pm Nov-Feb ⊖ Camden Town/Chalk Farm Ƌ good

Ragged School Museum (2, J3)

You up the back! Are you paying attention? This is partly a social history lesson about Dr J Barnado and the free schools he founded in the East End. But there's also a re-created Victorian classroom, where strict disciplinarians teach children the three Rs the old-fashioned way. Phone for lesson details and timings. ☎ 8980 6405 ▢ www .raggedschoolmuseum .org.uk ✉ 46-50 Copperfield Rd E3 £ free, donation requested ☼ 10am-5pm Wed-Thu & 2-5pm 1st Sun of month ⊖ Mile End

Woolwich Royal Arsenal (1, C1)

Firepower at the Woolwich Royal Arsenal re-creates the experiences of artillery gunners over the past century. It's loud, it flashes and the kids can't get enough. ☎ 8855 7755 ▢ www .firepower.org.uk ✉ Royal Arsenal Woolwich SE18 £ £6.50/4.50-5.50 ☼ 10am-5pm ⊞ Woolwich Arsenal Ƌ excellent

City Farms

For a touch of rural life and the sight of real live farm animals in the middle of a metropolis, head for London's city farms. Pony rides and feeding the animals are among the activities on offer.

- **Hackney City Farm** (2, H2 ☎ 7729 6381; 1a Goldsmith's Row E2 ☼ 10am-4.30pm Tue-Sun ⊖ Bethnal Green)
- **Kentish Town City Farm** (2, D1 ☎ 7916 5420; 1 Cressfield Close, Grafton Rd NW5 ☼ 9.30am-5.30pm Tue-Sun ⊖ Kentish Town)
- **Surrey Docks Farm** (2, J4 ☎ 7231 1010; Rotherhithe St SE16 ☼ 9am-5pm Tue-Thu, 9am-1pm, 2-5pm Sat & Sun ⊖ Canada Water/Surrey Quays)

Out & About

WALKING TOURS
Whitehall Wander

Start at Prince Charles' residence, **St James's Palace** (**1**). Skirt round its eastern side down Marlborough Rd and emerge in **The Mall** (**2**), with **Buckingham Palace** (**3**; p23) to the southwest. Enter **St James's Park** (**4**; p37), cross the footbridge and follow the lake to its eastern end. Turn south (right) into Horse Guards Rd, past the **Cabinet War Rooms** (**5**; p30).

All lit up: Trafalgar Square, overlooking St Martin-in-the-Fields

Continue south and then turn east (left) into Great George St to Parliament Square and **Westminster Abbey** (**6**; p12). Across St Margaret St lie the **Houses of Parliament** (**7**; p13) with the famous clock tower, **Big Ben** (**8**; p13). Refuel at the **Westminster Arms pub-restaurant** (**9** ☎ 7222 8520; 9 Storey's Gate SW1), west across the square.

From Parliament Square, walk north towards Whitehall, lined with the grand buildings of government ministries. The house to the left with the black door at **No 10 Downing St** (**10**) has accommodated UK prime ministers since 1732. Further along on the right is **Banqueting House** (**11**), the last remnant of the Tudor Whitehall Palace. King Charles I, accused of treason by Cromwell, was beheaded outside the house on 30 January 1649.

Finally, you arrive in **Trafalgar Square** (**12**), with **Nelson's Column** (**13**) in the centre, the **National Gallery** (**14**; p14) and **National Portrait Gallery** (**15**; p16) to the north and **St Martin-in-the-Fields** (**16**; p35) to the northeast. To the southwest is **Admiralty Arch** (**17**), erected in honour of Queen Victoria in 1910.

distance 2.2 miles (3.5km)
duration 3hr
▶ **start** ⊖ Green Park
⬤ **end** ⊖ Charing Cross

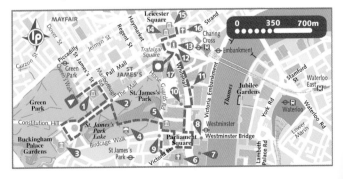

East End Amble

Emerging from the tube, have a look at the restored **Liverpool St train station** (**1**), featured in the Tom Cruise movie *Mission Impossible*. Cross the road and walk north, turning east into Folgate St, where you'll pass the quirky **Dennis Severs' House** (**2**; p39). Continue east and turn south (right) into Commercial St. On the right is the covered **Spitalfields Market** (**3**; p54), open on Sundays. To your right across Commercial St is the impressive **Christ Church, Spitalfields** (**4**), built by Sir Christopher Wren's protégé Nicholas Hawksmoor in 1729. To your left is the **Ten Bells pub** (**5** ☎ 7336 1721), where many of Jack the Ripper's victims used to drink.

Continue east along Fournier St, admiring the fine Georgian houses, where French Huguenot weavers fleeing religious persecution in their Catholic homeland lived in the 18th century.

At **Brick Lane** (**6**; p53) turn north (left), heading past its array of curry houses and shops selling bright fabrics, spices and Islamic religious items. At Nos 91–95 is the **Old Truman Brewery** (**7**), housing funky shops and the popular **Vibe Bar** (**8** ☎ 7377 2899). Further north is the famous **Brick Lane Beigel Bake** (**9** ☎ 7729 0616) at No 159.

Turn around and retrace your steps, continuing south to the end of Brick Lane at Whitechapel High St. Turn northeast (left) and continue along to the **Whitechapel Bell Foundry** (**10** ☎ 7247 2599; 32-34 Whitechapel Rd). This is where Big Ben (1858) and the Liberty Bell (1752; world-famous symbol of American independence), were cast (☺ prebooked 1½hr guided tour 10am Sat; £8).

All that ringing takes its toll

distance 1½ miles (2.5km)
duration 2hr
▶ **start** ⊖ Liverpool St
◉ **end** ⊖ Whitechapel

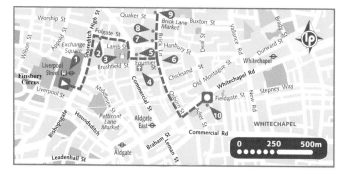

Fleet St Footslog

Begin at Ludgate Circus and walk west along Fleet St; on the southern (left) side is **St Bride's** (**1**; p35). Further along on the north (right) is Wine Office Court, an alleyway leading to **Ye Olde Cheshire Cheese pub** (**2**).

Continue west and turn north (right) into Dr Johnson's Court, leading to **Dr Johnson's House** (**3**; p38). A bit further along Fleet St on the southern side is **Ye Olde Cock Tavern** (**4**) at No 22, the oldest pub on Fleet St and a favourite of the good doctor, Pepys, Dickens and TS Eliot. Op-

Classic case of the old bended knees

distance 1.4 miles (2.2km)
duration 2½hr
▶ **start** ⊖ Blackfriars or St Paul's
● **end** ⊖ Charing Cross, Embankment or Temple (closed Sun)

posite stands **St Dunstan-in-the-West** (**5**), which narrowly escaped the Great Fire.

At No 17 is **Prince Henry's Room** (**6** ☎ 7936 2710; admission free ☺ 11am-2pm Mon-Sat), boasting London's best Jacobean plaster ceiling. The archway here leads to **Temple Church** (**7**; p35). The **griffin statue** (**8**) in the centre of Fleet St marks the site of the original Temple Bar, where the City of Westminster becomes the City of London and the Strand begins.

Some lovely old buildings line the southern footpath, including the **Wig & Pen Club** (**9**) at Nos 229–230. This is where journalists and lawyers would meet during civil (eg libel) court cases being held in the neo-Gothic **Royal Courts of Justice** (**10**), across the road. On the traffic island is **St Clement Danes church** (**11**) where at 9am, noon, 3pm and 6pm the bells chime 'Oranges and Lemons'. Further west is **St Mary-le-Strand** (**12**), while to the southwest is **Somerset House** (**13**; p29), with the marvellous Courtauld Gallery, Hermitage Rooms and Gilbert Collection.

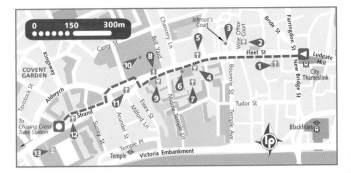

Docklands Dawdle

Begin at the **Tower of London** (**1**; p15) and walk east under **Tower Bridge** (**2**; p34) to **St Katharine's Dock** (**3**), the first of London's docks to be renovated (in 1968). East along the river from the dock, along St Katharine's Way, is **Wapping** (**4**). Cobbled Wapping High St leads past **Execution Dock** (**5**) at Wapping Stairs, where convicted pirates, including Captain William Kidd, were hanged and their bodies chained to a post at low tide.

Walk north along Wapping Lane and across to **St George-in-the-East** (**6**), designed by Nicholas Hawksmoor in 1726. Cannon St Rd leads to Cable St, where ropes were once made. Head east to the former **town hall building** (**7**) – now a library – which bears a mural marking the attempt by British Fascist Blackshirts to intimidate the local Jewish population in 1936. Enter the **Limehouse** (**8**) district by following Cable St east and north to Commercial Rd, where you'll find reminders of London's first Chinatown (which dates back to the 19th century) with names such as Ming and Mandarin Sts.

Head east to West India Dock Rd, leading south to the **Isle of Dogs** (**9**), which is dominated by Cesar Pelli's 244m steel-and-glass colossus **One Canada Square** (**10**), more commonly known as Canary Wharf Tower. The **Museum in Docklands** (**11**; p31) is across the channel to the north, in one of the old warehouses along West India Quay. After visiting the museum, enjoy a beer in a neighbouring bar, then head back to Canary Wharf Tower and the **Canary Wharf Underground station** (**12**). Designed by Sir Norman Foster in 2000, it's one of London's most impressive. Its scale is reminiscent of Fritz Lang's classic silent movie *Metropolis*, and it's an excellent starting point for exploring the **Jubilee line extension** (p39).

Tower Bridge: a neo-Gothic engineering feat

distance 4 miles (6.5km)
duration 3¾hr
▶ **start** ⊖ Tower Hill
◉ **end** ⊖ Canary Wharf

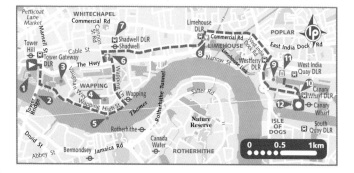

DAY TRIPS
Brighton (1, C3)

No wonder so many articles about London's favourite seaside resort go for the headline 'Brighton Rocks'. It first became popular when the dissolute Prince Regent (later King George IV) built his outrageous summer palace, the Royal Pavilion, here in the 18th century as a venue for lavish parties. And that charmingly seedy 'great-place-for-a-dirty-weekend' vibe lasted throughout the gang-ridden 1930s of Graham Greene's novel *Brighton Rock* and the mods versus rockers rivalry of the 1960s – think *Quadrophenia*. Today, an easy commute from London and a centre of English learning for foreign students, it's among the UK's hippest cities. Norman Cook (aka Fatboy Slim), Cate Blanchett, Julie Burchill and other media folk all live here, while a Frank (of Guggenheim Bilbao fame) Gehry building is planned for the waterfront.

Unfortunately, the city's historic West Pier partially collapsed in 2002, but tacky amusement rides still whirl on Brighton Pier. Buy a stick of hard, 'Brighton rock' candy and explore the trendy boutiques in the narrow streets called The Lanes.

INFORMATION

51 miles (82km) south of London

- 🚃 Victoria (40 fast trains daily, 50min); King's Cross Thameslink, Blackfriars & London Bridge (1hr)
- 🚌 National Express (hourly, 1hr 50min)
- 💻 www.visitbrighton.co.uk
- ℹ️ TIC (☎ 0906 711 2255; Bartholomew Sq); Royal Pavilion (☎ 01273-290900; Pavilion Pde; £5.80/3.40-4, family £15 🕙 10am-5pm last entry, to 4.30pm Oct-May 🚻 fair)
- ✖️ Terre à Terre (☎ 01273-729051; 71 East St)

Despite a name change, Brighton née Palace Pier is still primo for candy sticks, rides and clubs

Cambridge (1, C1)

While it lacks the evocative nickname of its rival Oxford – the city of dreaming spires – Cambridge is just as important and beautiful a university town. Who can resist the sentimental image of the nation's brightest cycling past in their gowns and mortarboards in the shadow of medieval and neo-Gothic buildings? Among the many high-profile figures who have worked and studied here are the discoverers of DNA, Watson and Crick (and Franklin), and tragic poets such as Sylvia Plath.

Although less touristy and manageable than Oxford, Cambridge – an architectural cornucopia – leaves its major colleges open to the public. That means you're generally free to explore the magnificent courts, chapels and libraries of Trinity College, St John's, King's and others. During exam time, however (mid-April to late June), they're often shut.

Take a Punt

Try that favourite Cambridge pastime of punting along the River Cam and hire a boat from **Trinity Punts** (☎ 01223-338483; Garret Hostel La; per hr £6, deposit £25) or **Scudamore's** (☎ 01223-359750; Grant Pl; per hr £12, £60 deposit). Chauffeured boat trips cost £6 to £10 per person.

INFORMATION

54 miles (87km) north of London

🚆 King's Cross St Pancras (every 30min, 1hr); Liverpool St (every 30min, 55min)

🚌 National Express (hourly, 2hr)

💻 www.cambridge.gov.uk

ℹ️ TIC (☎ 0906 586 2526 or 01223 457 574 for tours; Wheeler St near Market Sq; 2hr guided tours £7.85/4 🕑 1.30pm); Fitzwilliam Museum (☎ 01223-332923; www .fitzmuseum.cam.ac.uk; Trumpington St; free 🕑 10am-5pm Tue-Sat, 2.15-5pm Sun 🚻 good)

🍴 Browns (☎ 01223-461655; 23 Trumpington St)

The Fitzwilliam Museum, founded in 1816, features an important collection of ancient Egyptian sarcophagi and Greek and Roman art in its lower galleries and paintings and drawings upstairs, with works by Titian, Veronese and Rubens.

When I grow up, I want to be a gondolier (practising on the Cam, near King's College)

Hampton Court Palace (1, B2)

'The greatest palace in Britain' boasts the website for King Henry VIII's former riverside pad (1515), and once you visit it's difficult to disagree. It has one of the best medieval hammer-beam ceilings in the UK (the other being in the Houses of Parliament, see p13) the best Tudor Kitchens, renowned gardens and the world's most famous garden maze.

Stairs inside Anne Boleyn's Gateway lead up to Henry VIII's State Apartments and the Great Hall. Off the Great Watching Chamber is the Haunted Gallery, reportedly visited by the ghost of Henry's fifth wife, Catherine Howard. The kitchens have been fitted out as they might have been in Henry's day and the King's Apartments extensively restored.

Outside are the superb Privy Gardens (pictured below) and the half-mile-long (800m) hornbeam and yew maze, which was planted in 1690.

INFORMATION

9 miles (15km) west of London
- 🚉 Waterloo (every 30min)
- 🚢 Westminster Pier (☎ 7930 4721; www.wpsa.co.uk; 3 daily Apr-Sep/Oct, 3½hr)
- ☎ 0870 752 7777; www.hrp.org.uk
- £ £11.80/7.70-8.70, family £35, £1 discount for prebooking; Privy Gardens £4/2.50; maze £3.50/2.50
- 🕑 10.15am-5.15pm last entry Mon, 9.30am-5.15pm last entry Tue-Sun, 3.45pm last entry Nov-Mar

GUY MOBERLY

Windsor Castle (1, B2)

Standing on chalk bluffs overlooking the River Thames, Windsor Castle has been home to British royalty for over 900 years and is one of the great surviving medieval castles. Highlights are the restored State Apartments and St George's Chapel, a fine example of late Gothic architecture and packed with the tombs of royalty (including George III and Henry VIII). Windsor Castle is the royals' weekend residence and parts of the castle may be closed off then, as is St George's Chapel on Sunday.

In May and June, weather (and other events) permitting, you can witness the changing of the guard at 11am Monday to Saturday (alternate days Monday to Saturday the rest of the year).

INFORMATION

23 miles (37km) west of London
- 🚉 Waterloo to Riverside Station (every 30min, 55min); Paddington to Windsor Central Station (hourly, 30min)
- 🚌 Green Line bus (☎ 0870 608 7261; www.greenline.co.uk; 5-10 daily, 1hr)
- 🖥 www.the-royal-collection.org.uk
- ⓘ TIC (☎ 01753-743900; www.windsor.gov.uk; 24 High St); Castle (☎ 020 7766 7304; £12/6-10, family £30, all half-price when State Apartments closed 🕑 9.45am-4pm last entry, 3pm last entry Nov-Feb)
- 🍴 Francesco's (☎ 01753-863773; 53 Peascod St)

ORGANISED TOURS

Tour Guides

Association of Professional Tourist Guides

APTG members study for two years and take exams to be awarded the coveted Blue Badge, so they're the *crème de la crème*. You can decide your own itinerary or have it planned for you, but obviously it's more affordable if you're in a group.

☎ 7505 3073 ⌨ www.touristguides.org.uk £ half-/full day (English) £97/146, (other language) £112/175

Bicycle

London Bicycle Tour Company (3, F4)

On offer are two cycling tours: the East tour (which takes in the Globe Theatre, Tower Bridge, Tobacco Dock, the East End proper, the City and St Paul's Cathedral); and the Royal West tour (which takes in the Houses of Parliament, Lambeth Palace, Kensington and Chelsea, the Royal Albert Hall, Buckingham Palace, St James's, Trafalgar Square and Covent Garden). Each tours lasts for three to 3½ hours.

☎ 7928 6838 ⌨ www.londonbicycle.com ✉ 1a Gabriel's Wharf, 56 Upper Ground SE1 £ incl bike £14.95 ☼ East tour 2pm Sat, Royal West tour 2pm Sun

Boat

City Cruises (3, D5)

City Cruises operates a year-round ferry service from Westminster Pier to Tower Pier and Tower Pier to

Guided Walks

Time Out's Around Town: Listings' section outlines what's on offer. Some popular themes are the Beatles' Magical Mystery Tour, Jewish London and, inevitably, a tour in the footsteps of Jack the Ripper through Whitechapel. Walks take about two hours and cost around £5/4 adult/concession.

These companies offer guided walks:

- **Citisights** (☎ 8806 4325; www.chr.org.uk/cswalks.htm)
- **Historical Tours** (☎ 8668 4019; www.historicalwalksoflondon.com)
- **London Walks** (☎ 7624 3978; www.walks.com)
- **Mystery Tours** (☎ 8558 9446; mysterywalks@hotmail.com)

Greenwich in a continuous loop that allows passengers to jump on and off at various stops. Boats depart every 20 to 40 minutes, with later departures in summer and fewer sailings in winter.

☎ 7740 0400 ⌨ www.citycruises.com ✉ Westminster Pier SW1 £ £8.70/4.25, family £23 ☼ 10am-4.30pm, later in Jun-Aug, fewer sailings Nov-Mar

London Waterbus Company (4, B2)

The London Waterbus Company runs 90-minute trips on Regent's Canal in an enclosed canal barge between Camden Lock and Little Venice, passing through Regent's Park and London Zoo along the way.

☎ 7482 2660 (information), 7482 2550 (bookings) ⌨ www.londonwaterbus.com ✉ 2 Middle Yard, Camden Lock NW1 £ single

£4.80/3.10, return £6.20/4 ☼ 10am-5pm (hourly, every 30min Sun) Apr-Oct, 10am-3/4pm (hourly) weekends only Nov-Mar

Westminster Passenger Services Association (3, D5)

WPSA riverboats go upriver from Westminster Pier to the Royal Botanic Gardens at Kew (1½ hours) and Hampton Court Palace (3½ hours), generally from late March/April to September/October. Phone or consult the website for exact schedules.

☎ 7930 4721 ⌨ www.wpsa.co.uk ✉ Westminster Pier SW1 £ Kew single £9/4.50-6, return £15/7.50-10; Hampton Court Palace single £12/6-8, return £18/9-12 ☼ Kew (via Putney) 10.15am-2pm (5 sailings) late Mar-Sep/Oct; Hampton Court Palace 10.30am, 11.15am, noon Apr-Sep/Oct

Bus
Original London Sightseeing Tour
The best known of London's many sightseeing bus companies, this one passes the main sights in double-decker buses, allowing you to hop on and off along the way and reboard the next bus. Convenient starting points are Trafalgar Square; in front of Baker St tube station next to Madame Tussaud's; on Haymarket southeast of Piccadilly Circus; Marble Arch (Speakers' Corner); and in Grosvenor Gardens opposite Victoria station.
☎ 8877 1722 🖳 www .theoriginaltour.com £ £15/10 🕒 9am-7/8pm summer, 9/9.30am-5/6pm winter

Helicopter
Cabair Helicopters
Cabair Helicopters offers 30-minute helicopter 'flight-seeing' tours over London every Sunday.
☎ 8953 4411 🖳 www.cabair.com ✉ Elstree Aerodrome, Borehamwood, Hertfordshire £ £129

The whizz-bang taxi tour

Not Quite Venice
London's 40 miles (65km) of inner-city canals, most of which were constructed for industry in the early 19th century, are being given a new lease of life as leisure resources. The 2½ mile-long (4km) Regent's Canal (4, A3), looping around north London from Little Venice in Maida Vale to Camden Lock, passing near London Zoo and Regent's Park, is a popular route for boating tour groups. For more details, contact **Waterfront** (☎ 01923-201101; www.waterscape .com), a part of British Waterways.

Specialist Tours
Black Taxi Tours of London
Exploiting perfectly the London cabbie's tendency to mouth off on any subject, a driver guide takes you on a two-hour spin past the major sights. Up to five people fit in one black taxi.
☎ 7935 9363 🖳 www .blacktaxitours.co.uk £ 8am-6pm £75, 6pm-midnight £85

London Duck Tours
(3, E5)
Seated in amphibious landing craft based on the design first used in the D-day landings in WWII, you cruise the streets of central London before making a dramatic plunge into the Thames.
☎ 7928 3132 🖳 www.londonduck tours.co.uk ✉ departing from County Hall £ £16.50/11-13, family £49 🕒 10am-6pm

Tours around London
Astral Tours
Themed tours (eg Shakespeare, Jane Austen's England, King Arthur and Celtic culture) cover one or more of the following: Bath, the Cotswolds, Leeds, Oxford, Salisbury, Avebury, Glastonbury and Stratford-upon-Avon. There's also a special tour where you are allowed inside the roped-off area of Stonehenge. The Astral minibus generally picks up from customers' hotels. Prices include all admission fees.
☎ 0700 078 1016, 0870 902 0908 🖳 www .astraltravels.co.uk £ day trip £49-65

Golden Tours (3, B6)
This company offers coach excursions with pick-ups from 65 London hotels to a great number of destinations, including Althorp (the final resting place of Diana, princess of Wales), Windsor, Hampton Court Gardens, Oxford, Stratford, Bath and Stonehenge.
☎ 7233 7030 🖳 www .goldentours.co.uk ✉ 4 Fountain Sq, 123-151 Buckingham Palace Rd SW1 £ half-day trip to Windsor & Runnymede £32/28, incl admission to castle; to Althorp £48/42

Shopping

'My brother (sister/mother/boyfriend etc) went to London and all I got was this lousy T-shirt.' Now, come on, you wouldn't want to limit your capital shopping to that infamous souvenir, would you?

It's not quite correct to say that if you can't find something in this retail mecca, it doesn't exist. However, there *are* hours of fun to be had in rummaging through the city's myriad consumer delights – whether you're looking for Harrods' English breakfast tea, something from Burberry, a Savile Row suit or hip streetwear.

Theme park for tourists (aka Harrods, p52)

True, London rarely offers the value found in New York but it's ever willing to encourage consumer spending. Shops generally open from 9am or 10am to 6pm or 7pm Monday to Saturday, with Sunday and late-night trading to 8pm or 9pm in Covent Garden, Oxford St and Soho (Thursday), plus Chelsea, Knightsbridge and Kensington (Wednesday).

Apart from some stalls at its fabulous weekend markets, credit cards are universally accepted. In short, if you're after retail therapy, the UK capital offers a great big sympathetic couch.

Shopping Areas

Tourists generally head for crowded Oxford St and Covent Garden in the West End. But apart from a few gems including Topshop and Selfridges, Oxford St usually disappoints. (High St Kensington and the ritzy King's Rd provide more comfortable alternatives.) On the other hand, away from the twee market in Covent Garden, there are interesting fashion, homewares and food boutiques on Floral St, including Monmouth Gardens, Shorts Gardens, Neal St and Neal's Yard.

Regent St is home to Liberty, Hamleys and a couple of classic English brands such as Aquascutum. Those with real cash will head to Bond St, Sloane St or Knightsbridge for designer labels such as Burberry, Nicole Farhi, Emporio Armani, DKNY, Gucci, Prada and Louis Vuitton. Those more interested in street cred might prefer a trip to Hoxton or Clerkenwell.

West End Buys

Some streets are known for particular specialities:

- **Bond St** – designer clothes and accessories
- **Cecil Court** – antiquarian bookshops
- **Charing Cross Rd** – new and second-hand books
- **Denmark St** – sheet music, books about music, musical instruments
- **Hanway St** – used records
- **Savile Row** – bespoke men's tailoring
- **Tottenham Court Rd** – electronics/computer equipment and homewares

DEPARTMENT STORES

Some London department stores are attractions in their own right, including Harrods, Fortnum & Mason and – ever since the cult TV series *Absolutely Fabulous* – 'Harvey Nicks' (Harvey Nichols).

Fortnum & Mason (6, B4)
You don't have to be Scott heading to the Antarctic to indulge in the famous food hampers, cut marmalade or unusual foodstuffs from the old-world food hall, though this is where the explorer came for supplies. Clothes take up the other six floors.
☎ 7734 8040 ⌨ www .fortnumandmason.co.uk ✉ 181 Piccadilly W1 ☼ 10am-6.30pm Mon-Sat ⊖ Piccadilly Circus

Harrods (2, D5)
This store is so famous it made its owner, Mohammed Al-Fayed, a global celebrity. It's a theme park for fans of the British establishment, where tourists move slowly past the souvenirs or swoon over the fabulous food halls. Watches and bags are found in the ground-floor Luxury Room, and don't miss the over-the-top opulence of the Egyptian Hall.
☎ 7730 1234 ⌨ www.harrods.com ✉ 87-135 Brompton Rd SW1 ☼ 10am-7pm Mon-Sat ⊖ Knightsbridge

Harvey Nichols (3, A5)
The city's temple of high fashion has a great 5th-floor food hall, extravagant perfume and jewellery departments, and all the big names – from Versace to Alexander McQueen.
☎ 7235 5000 ⌨ www .harveynichols.com ✉ 109-125 Knights-bridge SW1 ☼ 10am-7pm Mon-Sat, to 8pm Wed-Fri, noon-6pm Sun ⊖ Knightsbridge

John Lewis (3, B3)
'Never knowingly undersold' is the motto of this store, whose range of household goods, fabrics and luggage is better described as reliable rather than cutting-edge.
☎ 7629 7711 ⌨ www.johnlewis.co.uk ✉ 278-306 Oxford St W1 ☼ 9.30am-7pm Mon-Fri, to 8pm Thu, 9am-6pm Sat ⊖ Oxford Circus

Liberty (6, A2)
Behind the mock Tudor façade you'll find the inimitable Liberty silk scarves and printed fabrics. There's

also upmarket fashion, plus refurbished cosmetic and lingerie departments.
☎ 7734 1234 ⌨ www.liberty.co.uk ✉ 210-220 Regent St W1 ☼ 10am-6.30pm Mon-Wed, to 8pm Thu, to 7pm Fri-Sat, noon-6pm Sun ⊖ Oxford Circus

Marks & Spencer (3, A3)
M&S is almost as British as fish and chips, beans on toast and warm beer. Despite the store's few forays into 'fashion', most people still shop here for good, sensible underwear.
☎ 7935 7954 ⌨ www .marksandspencer.com ✉ 458 Oxford St W1 ☼ 9am-8pm Mon-Fri, 9am-7pm Sat, noon-6pm Sun ⊖ Marble Arch

Selfridges (3, A3)
The funkiest and most vital of London's one-stop shops, famous for its window displays, Selfridges is a huge temple to Mammon. There are excellent food halls, make-up and perfume counters, and vast arrays of clothing and accessories, including DKNY, Joseph, Marc Jacobs, Prada, Anna Hindmarch handbags and purses by Antoni & Alison.
☎ 7629 1234 ⌨ www.selfridges.co.uk ✉ 400 Oxford St W1 ☼ 10am-7pm Mon-Wed, to 8pm Thu-Fri, 9.30am-7pm Sat, noon-6pm Sun ⊖ Bond Street

Sales Fever

Camping overnight in the cold, a crush of punters elbowing each other in the daytime crush, and celebrity guest appearances – are we talking about the Glastonbury rock festival? No, this is what happens during the biannual London sales, in January and July, when queues form outside department stores, sometimes starting the night before. Pack a sleeping bag if you wish to join in.

MARKETS

Bermondsey (3, J6)
Local lore has it that, before 8am, this is the place to go for goods that may have fallen off the back of a truck. So you can come here not only for furnishing and other curios, but also for an early morning taste of cockney-style 'ducking and diving' (avoiding the law, living hand-to-mouth).

☎ 7969 1500
✉ Bermondsey Sq, cnr Bermondsey St & Long La SE1 🕑 5am-1pm Fri
⊖ Borough/Bermondsey

Brixton (2, F6)
Reggae plays in the back-ground, incense wafts on the air and the eyes are greeted by the vibrant colours of Afri-can prints and Rastafarian hats in this urban British slice of Africa/Latin-America/the Caribbean. Foodstuffs – eg goat meat, tilapia fish, exotic fruits, spices and sugar cane – and homeopathic root cures are also on sale, especially in Electric Avenue and covered Granville Arcade.
✉ Reliance & Granville Arcades, Market Row, Electric La & Electric Ave SW9 🕑 8am-6pm Mon-Tue & Thu-Sat, 8am-3pm Wed ⊖ Brixton

Camden (4, B2)
Although – or perhaps because – it stopped being cutting-edge several thou-sand cheap leather jackets ago, this is one of London's top tourists attractions and its most popular market. Things peak on weekends, when crowds snake slowly along the littered streets, but

Botero makes it big at Bermondsey

shops are open most days. There are several sections, all merging into one. The Stables, near the Chalk Farm end, is generally thought to be the best part, with its mix of antiques, Asian artefacts, rugs and carpets, pine furniture, and '50s and '60s clothing.
✉ Camden High St & Chalk Farm Rd NW1 🕑 10am-6pm Sat & Sun ⊖ Camden Town

To Market, to Market
Other interesting markets near central London are:
- **Berwick St** (6, C2 🕑 8am-6pm Mon-Sat ⊖ Piccadilly Circus/Oxford Circus) Fruit and vegetables.
- **Brick Lane** (3, J2 🕑 8am-1pm Sun ⊖ Aldgate East) Cheap continental cigarettes are the speciality, along with clothes, food, household goods and other bric-a-brac.
- **Borough** (3, H5; cnr Borough High & Stoney Sts 🕑 9am-6pm Fri, 9am-4pm Sat ⊖ London Bridge) Jamie Oliver is the most famous customer at this pukkah foodies' market.
- **Columbia Rd** (3, J1 🕑 7am-1pm Sun ⊖ Bethnal Green 🚇 Cambridge Heath or 🚌 26, 48 or 55) A wonderfully perfumed avenue of flowers and plants.
- **Leadenhall** (3, H3; Whittington Ave, off Grace-church St EC1 🕑 7am-4pm Mon-Fri ⊖ Bank) Fresh fish, meat and cheese are sold in this faux-Victorian alley, featured in *Harry Potter and the Philosopher's Stone* (*Sorcerer's Stone*, US).
- **Smithfield** (3, F3; West Smithfield EC1 🕑 4am-noon Mon-Fri ⊖ Farringdon) Central London's last surviving meat market.

VAT

Value-added tax (VAT) is a 17.5% sales tax levied on most goods (except food, books and children's clothing) and services in the UK. Non-EU citizens can sometimes get a VAT refund on goods they take home. Not all shops participate in the refund scheme, and minimum-purchase conditions vary (normally around £75). Ask for details when making a purchase.

Covent Garden (6, E2)

While the shops in the Covent Garden Piazza are open daily, a couple of markets also take place here. The better one is the Apple Market in the North Hall with quality crafts sold daily. On Monday an antiques and bric-a-brac market is held in Jubilee Hall on the southern side of the piazza; during the rest of the week it's full of schlock.

✉ **Covent Garden Piazza WC2** ⏲ **Apple Market 9am-5pm; Jubilee Market 9am-3pm Mon, 9am-5pm Tue-Sun** ⊖ **Covent Garden**

Greenwich (5, B2)

Greenwich generally is great for retro clothing and the undercover market here specialises in decorated glass, rugs, prints, wooden toys and other craft items. There are also antiques and curios on Thursday.

✉ **College Approach, King William Walk & Greenwich Church St SE10** ⏲ **9.30am-5.30pm Wed & Fri-Sun, 9am-5pm Thu** ⚆ **DLR Cutty Sark**

Petticoat Lane (3, J3)

Despite its renown and alluring moniker, Petticoat Lane has been reduced to run-of-the-mill trash, where tourists lose themselves in a forest of cheap T-shirts and trainers.

✉ **Middlesex & Wentworth Sts E1** ⏲ **8am-2pm Sun (Wentworth St only 9am-2pm Mon-Fri)** ⊖ **Liverpool St**

Portobello Road (2, B4)

London's second most popular market after Camden, Portobello Rd wends its way from Notting Hill Gate to the Westway flyover in Ladbroke Grove. Antiques, handmade jewellery, paintings and ethnic stuff are concentrated at the Notting Hill Gate end, before you move into fruit and vegetables, second-hand clothing, cheap household goods and general junk. Though a few shops and stalls open daily, Friday to Sunday is busiest for clothes. There's also an antiques market on Saturday and a flea market on Portobello Green Sunday morning.

✉ **Portobello Rd W10** ⏲ **8am-6pm Mon-Wed, 9am-1pm Thu, 7am-7pm Fri, 6am-5pm Sat, 6am-2pm Sun** ⊖ **Notting Hill Gate/Ladbroke Grove/ Westbourne Park**

Spitalfields (3, J2)

Its hip, Hoxton-side location and its relative newness compared to Camden and Portobello make Spitalfields the favourite market of many young Londoners. Inside its huge Victorian warehouse, clothes by upcoming designers, retro furniture, organic candles and ethnic knick-knacks sit alongside food stalls turning out Thai, Turkish and other cuisines. Sometimes there are fresh coconuts and inevitably, ugh, wheatgrass shots. An organic produce market takes place on Friday.

✉ **Commercial St E1** ⏲ **9.30am-5.30pm Sun** ⊖ **Liverpool St/Shoreditch**

Got a weakness for wheatgrass? Head to Spitalfields.

CLOTHING & ACCESSORIES

Agent Provocateur (6, C2)
For women's lingerie to die for (or over, or in), check out this decidedly window-shoppable place.
☎ 7439 0229 🖳 www
.agentprovocateur.com
✉ 6 Broadwick St W1
🕑 11am-7pm Mon-Sat
⊖ Oxford Circus

Aquascutum (6, B3)
Did we mention it rains a bit in London? Never fear. The retro-inspired pea jackets and storm coats at this bastion of British design will help you withstand the elements.
☎ 7675 8200 🖳 www
.aquascutum.co.uk ✉ 100
Regent St W1 🕑 10am-6.30pm Mon-Sat, to 7pm Thu, noon-5pm Sun
⊖ Piccadilly Circus

Burberry (6, A3)
Home of the tartan-lined mackintosh, Burberry is still enjoying a renaissance as a trendy brand. Its bags, coats, skirts, shirts, jumpers and accessories are available

cut-price at the **Burberry Factory Shop** (2, J1
☎ 8985 3344; 29 Chatham Palace E9 🚇 Hackney Central or ⊖ Bethnal Green, then bus106 or 256 to Hackney Town Hall)
☎ 7839 5222 ✉ 21-23 New Bond St SW1
🕑 10am-7pm Mon-Sat, noon-6pm Sun ⊖ Bond St/Oxford Circus

Cyberdog (6, D2)
Cyberdog's fluorescent-print T-shirts, cool trousers and other cult wear make it an essential stop before that important clubbing night.
☎ 7836 7855 🖳 www
.cyberdog.net ✉ 9 Earlham St WC2 🕑 11am-7pm Mon-Sat, noon-6pm Sun ⊖ Covent Garden

Duffer of St George (6, E1)
Shirts and classic Italian suits sit alongside branded jeans and T-shirts at Duffer, the meisters of London menswear.
☎ 7836 3722 🖳 www
.thedufferofstgeorge.com

✉ 29 Shorts Gardens WC2 🕑 10am-7pm Mon-Fri, 10.30am-6.30pm Sat, 1-5pm Sun ⊖ Covent Garden

High Jinks (6, D2)
This large streetwear emporium is crammed full of street fashion, for men and women, made by young designers.
☎ 7240 5580 🖳 www
.high-jinks.com ✉ Thomas Neal Centre, Earlham St WC2 🕑 10am-7pm Mon-Sat, noon-6pm Sun
⊖ Covent Garden

James Smith & Sons (6, D1)
Jam-packed with umbrellas, canes and walking sticks behind its half-mirrored exterior, this shop is caught in its own little time warp of quintessential Englishness.
☎ 7836 4731 🖳 www
.james-smith.co.uk
✉ 53 New Oxford St WC1 🕑 9.30am-5.25pm Mon-Fri, 10am-5.25pm Sat ⊖ Holborn/Tottenham Court Rd

CLOTHING & SHOE SIZES

Women's Clothing

Aust/UK	8	10	12	14	16	18
Europe	36	38	40	42	44	46
Japan	5	7	9	11	13	15
USA	6	8	10	12	14	16

Women's Shoes

Aust/USA	5	6	7	8	9	10
Europe	35	36	37	38	39	40
France only	35	36	38	39	40	42
Japan	22	23	24	25	26	27
UK	3½	4½	5½	6½	7½	8½

Men's Clothing

Aust	92	96	100	104	108	112
Europe	46	48	50	52	54	56

Japan	S	M	M		L	
UK/USA	35	36	37	38	39	40

Men's Shirts (Collar Sizes)

Aust/Japan	38	39	40	41	42	43
Europe	38	39	40	41	42	43
UK/USA	15	15½	16	16½	17	17½

Men's Shoes

Aust/UK	7	8	9	10	11	12
Europe	41	42	43	44½	46	47
Japan	26	27	27.5	28	29	30
USA	7½	8½	9½	10½	11½	12½

Measurements approximate only; try before you buy.

On the High Street

Overseas retailers, such as the Gap, H & M, Mambo, Mango, Morgan, Muji and Zara, abound. The UK also has many home-grown clothing chains, including:

- **French Connection UK** (3, A3 ☎ 7629 7766; 396 Oxford St W1 ⊖ Bond St) Clothes more sober than the FCUK sobriquet suggests.
- **Jigsaw** (3, B3 ☎ 7491 4484; 126-127 New Bond St W1 ⊖ Bond St) Classic women's clothes grouped together by colour.
- **Karen Millen** (6, E2 ☎ 7836 5355; 32-33 James St WC2 ⊖ Covent Garden) A tasteful take on figure-hugging frocks and glam trouser suits.
- **Miss Selfridge** (6, A1 ☎ 7927 0188; 325 Oxford St ⊖ Oxford Circus) Fun, throwaway fashion for teen girls.
- **Oasis** (6, E2 ☎ 7240 7445; 13 James St WC2 ⊖ Covent Garden) Where Topshop (see below) customers go when they and their wallets grow up.
- **Office** (6, E2 ☎ 7379 1896; 57 Neal St WC2 ⊖ Covent Garden) Shoes that go the distance from work to after-hours drinks.
- **Shellys** (6, A1 ☎ 7287 0939; 266-270 Regent St W1 ⊖ Oxford Circus) For funky-looking, colourful footwear.
- **Topshop & Topman** (6, A1 ☎ 7636 7700; 36-38 Great Castle St W1, entrance Oxford St ⊖ Oxford Circus) Both teenagers and trendy parents love the reasonably priced interpretations of the latest catwalk fashions.
- **Warehouse** (6, E2 ☎ 7240 8242; 24 Long Acre WC2 ⊖ Covent Garden/ Leicester Sq) Somewhere between Topshop and Oasis in the fashion stakes.

Koh Samui (6, D2)
As lovely and ethereal as this upmarket boutique might leave you feeling, it's hard to imagine wearing the likes of Antoni Berardi, Clements Ribeiro or Julien MacDonald on the Thai island of the title.
☎ 7240 4280 ⊠ 65-67 Monmouth St WC2

Post-modern eye patches

🕒 10am-6.30pm Mon-Sat, from 10.30am Wed & Fri, 11am-5.30pm Sun ⊖ Leicester Sq

Laden Showrooms (3, J2)
This is the best barometer of trendy Hoxton fashion, with zippered men's T-shirts, ribboned 1950s A-line skirts, or whatever happens to be in on London's streets.
☎ 7247 2431 ⌨ www .laden.co.uk ⊠ 103 Brick La E1 🕒 noon-6pm Mon-Fri, 10.30am-6pm Sat & Sun ⊖ Liverpool St

Paul Smith (6, E2)
Cleverly cut and very wear-able men's and women's lines have made Sir Paul one of the most sought after Brit designers.
☎ 7379 7133 ⌨ www.paulsmith.co.uk

⊠ 40-44 Floral St WC2 🕒 10.30am-6.30pm Mon-Fri, to 7pm Thu, 10am-6.30 Sat, 1-5pm Sun ⊖ Covent Garden

Pringle (3, B4)
Taking a leaf from Burberry's book, stately Pringle has turned golfers' jumpers into something hip by slashing necklines to the waist and using lots of pink. Accessories include brilliantly comfortable sleep masks.
☎ 0800 360 200 ⌨ www.pringle-of-scotland.co.uk ⊠ 112 New Bond St W1 🕒 10am-7pm Mon-Sat, noon-6pm Sun ⊖ Bond St

Rigby & Peller (2, D5)
Impress those back home with a properly fitted bra,

corset or swimming costume made by the Queen's very own corsetière.

☎ 7589 9293 🖳 www .rigbyandpeller.com ✉ 2 Hans Rd SW3 🕑 10am-6pm Mon-Sat, to 7pm Wed ⊖ Knightsbridge

Stella McCartney (6, A3)
If you're not like Stella's friends Madonna, Gwyneth and Kate (Moss) in being able to afford £1000 for a corset dress, her opulent store is still a stunning browse in itself.

☎ 7518 3100 🖳 www .stellamccartney.com ✉ 30 Bruton St W1 🕑 10am-6pm Mon-Sat, to 7pm Thu ⊖ Green Park

Urban Outfitters (6, E2)
The American chain has made a big splash in London with its cool streetwear labels for gals and guys, saucy women's underwear, funky homewares and quirky gadgets. There is a branch at 36-38 High St, Kensington (2, C4).

☎ 7759 6390 🖳 www .urbanoutfitters.com ✉ Seven Dials House, 42-56 Earlham St WC2 🕑 10am-7pm Mon-Sat, to 8pm Thu, noon-6pm Sun ⊖ Covent Garden

Vivienne Westwood (3, B4)
Age has not withered her. The original godmother of punk fashion, now an OBE,

continues to mix the radical with the historical in her schizophrenic women's and menswear.

☎ 7629 3757 ✉ 6 Davies St W1 🕑 10am-6pm Mon-Sat, to 7pm Thu ⊖ Bond St

Tartan it up, Burberry (p54)

JEWELLERY

Garrard (6, A3)
Creative director Jade Jagger (yes, Mick's daughter) helped turn an old-fashioned jeweller's into somewhere funky enough for Missy Elliott to advertise its bling, bling. Jewel-encrusted clothing and gifts are sold upstairs.

☎ 7758 8520 🖳 www .garrard.com ✉ 24 Albermarle St W1 🕑 10am-5.30pm Mon-Sat ⊖ Bond St/Green Park

Mappin & Webb (6, B3)
Since 1774 this business has been a favourite haunt for those hunting out corporate gifts. But customers with no time to wait for something bespoken or engraved can pick up designer watches or other

off-the-shelf trinkets.

☎ 7734 3801 🖳 www .mappin-and-webb.co.uk ✉ 170 Regent St W1 🕑 10am-6pm Mon-Sat, to 7pm Thu ⊖ Oxford Circus/Piccadilly Circus

Wright & Teague (6, A4)
These two stars from 1980s

Central St Martins College of Art & Design continue to turn out original but elegant gold and silver pieces.

☎ 7629 2777 🖳 www .wrightandteague.com ✉ 1A Grafton St W1 🕑 10am-6pm Mon-Fri, to 7pm Thu, 10am-5pm Sat ⊖ Green Park

Diamond Cluster

Clerkenwell is a hot spot for jewellery, both traditional and modern. For classic settings and un-mounted stones, head to **Hatton Garden** EC1 (3, F2 ⊖ Chancery La/Farringdon). Five minutes away is the **Lesley Craze Gallery** (3, F2 ☎ 7608 0393; 33-35a Clerkenwell Green EC1 ⊖ Farringdon), one of Europe's leading centres for contemporary jewellery. **Ec one** (3, F1 ☎ 7713 6185; www.econe.co.uk; 41 Exmouth Market EC1 ⊖ Farringdon) has some funky pieces favoured by Hollywood stars such as Cameron Diaz.

DESIGN, ARTS & CRAFTS

Conran Shop (2, C5)
The sort of china you find in the many Conran restaurants is joined by furniture, kitchen and bath accessories in this lifestyle emporium. It's worth the visit for the stunning Michelin building alone.
☎ 7589 7401 ▢ www .conran.com ✉ Michelin House, 81 Fulham Rd, Chelsea SW3 ⏱ 10am-6pm Mon-Fri, to 7pm Wed-Thu, 10am-6.30pm

Bitchin' interior design

Sat, noon-6pm Sun
⊖ South Kensington

Eat My Handbag Bitch (3, J2)
Despite the name, there's not a handbag in sight here, just retro furniture and general 20th-century design classics, including chairs, lamps and vases.
☎ 7375 3100 ▢ www. eatmyhandbagbitch.co.uk ✉ Old Truman Brewery, 6 Dray Walk, 91-95 Brick La E1 ⏱ 10am-6pm ⊖ Liverpool St/Shoreditch

Habitat (3, C2)
Don't be fooled by the young urban dwellers who unfairly nickname this place 'Shabby tat'; they're the first to snaffle its reasonably priced, but still fashionable, homewares.
☎ 7631 3880 ▢ www .habitat.net ✉ 196 Tottenham Court Rd W1 ⏱ 10am-6pm Mon-Wed, to 8pm Thu, to 6.30pm

Fri, 9.30am-6.30pm
Sat, noon-6pm Sun
⊖ Goodge St

Heals (3, C2)
This 200-year-old institution is more upmarket than Habitat. Exclusive and seriously good quality tables, linen, furnishings, rugs etc line its shopfront windows and the floors behind.
☎ 7636 1666 ▢ www.heals.co.uk ✉ 196 Tottenham Court Rd W1 ⏱ 10am-6pm Mon-Wed, to 8pm Thu, to 6.30pm Fri, 9.30am-6.30pm Sat, noon-6pm Sun ⊖ Goodge St

Purves & Purves (3, C2)
Here you'll find the same quality furnishings, lighting, kitchenware and accessories you'd get at Heals but in more colourful, avant-garde mode – think Alessi kettles and Ritzenhoff mugs. It's also great for gifts.
☎ 7580 8223 ▢ www .purves.co.uk ✉ 220-224 Tottenham Court Rd W1 ⏱ 9.30am-6pm Mon-Sat, from 10am Tue, to 7pm Thu, 11.30am-5.30pm Sun ⊖ Goodge St

Royal Doulton (6, B3)
All of 175 years old and still churning out traditional porcelain figures and tableware, this classic English firm has introduced funkier designs in glassware and cutlery.
☎ 7734 3184 ▢ www .royal-doulton.com ✉ 154 Regent St W1 ⏱ 10am-6pm Mon-Sat, to 7pm Thu, 11am-5pm Sun ⊖ Piccadilly Circus

Going, Going, Gone!
A visit to one of London's auction houses is a chance to see a great institution at work. However, don't fidget while things go under the hammer or you might unexpectedly find yourself the proud owner of an old master or something equally costly!

- **Bonhams** (2, C5 ☎ 7393 3900; www.bonhams.com; Montpelier St SW7 ⊖ Knightsbridge)
- **Christie's** (3,C5 ☎ 7839 9060; www.christies.com; 8 King St SW1 ⊖ Green Park/Piccadilly Circus)
- **Phillips** (3, B3 ☎ 7629 6602; www.phillips-auctions.com; 101 New Bond St W1 ⊖ Bond St)
- **Sotheby's** (6, A3 ☎ 7293 5000; www.sothebys.com; 34-35 New Bond St W1 ⊖ Bond St)

ANTIQUES

Antique hunters may also find something worthwhile at the Saturday antiques market along Portobello Rd (p54) or Bermondsey Market (p53).

Camden Passage (2, F2)
Confusingly located in Islington, despite the name, these four arcades of antique shops are primarily aimed at professional dealers. Stall-holders know their stuff and real bargains are a rarity.
☎ 7359 0190 ⌧ Upper St & Essex Rd N1 ⏱ 7.30am- 2pm Wed, 8am-4pm Sat ⊖ Angel

Grays Antiques Market (3, B4)
Antique jewellery is the speciality here, while the

nearby Davies Mews have dolls, glass and porcelain.
☎ 7629 7034 ⌨ www .egrays.com ⌧ 58 Davies St W1 ⏱ 10am-6pm Mon-Fri ⊖ Bond St

Lassco (3, H2)
Architectural salvage company Lassco has stocked a disused church with everything from small curios to slate tiles, oak floorboards, marble fireplaces and garden ornaments.
☎ 7749 9944 ⌨ www .lassco.co.uk ⌧ St

Michael's Church, Mark St EC2 ⏱ 10am-5pm Mon-Sat, to 8pm Tue ⊖ Old St

London Silver Vaults (3, E3)
These 40 subterranean shops in Chancery House are home to one of the world's largest collections of silver. The metal comes in many forms, from jewellery and picture frames to candelabras and tea services for 12.
☎ 7242 3844 ⌧ 53-63 Chancery La WC2 ⏱ 9am-5.30pm Mon-Fri, 9am-1pm Sat ⊖ Chancery La

MUSIC

It's not for nothing that the musically obsessed novel *High Fidelity* was set in London (unlike the Chicago-based film). Even if you ignored – as many purists do – the monolithic outlets such as **HMV Records** (6, B1 ☎ 7631 3423; 150 Oxford St W1 ⊖ Oxford Circus) and the **Virgin Megastore** (6, C1 ☎ 7631 1234; 14-30 Oxford St W1 ⊖ Tottenham Court Rd), this city has musical product coming out of its ears.

Blackmarket Records (6, B2)
This is where DJs flock for the latest club dance music. After all, who can resist a place with a lower-level 'drum and bassment'?
☎ 7437 0478 ⌨ www .blackmarket .co.uk ⌧ 25 D'Arblay St W1 ⏱ noon-7pm Mon, 11am-7pm Tue-Sat ⊖ Oxford Circus

Honest Jon's (2, B3)
This legendary shop – where DJ James Lavelle was once an assistant and which runs a record label with Damon Albarn – is renowned for its wide range of jazz, reggae,

rarities, reissues and 12in vinyl records.
☎ 8969 9822 ⌨ www .honestjons.com ⌧ 276 & 278 Portobello Rd W10 ⏱ 10am-6pm Mon-Sat, 11am-5pm Sun ⊖ Ladbroke Grove

Mole Jazz (3, D1)
Two floors of vinyl, tapes and CDs – probably the best shop for old-style jazz in London.
☎ 7278 8623 ⌨ www .molejazz.co.uk ⌧ 311 Gray's Inn Rd WC1 ⏱ 10am-6pm Mon-Sat, to 8pm Fri ⊖ King's Cross St Pancras

Reckless Records (6, B2)
New and second-hand records and CDs run the gamut from punk, soul, dance, independent and mainstream.
☎ 7437 4271 ⌨ www.reckless.co.uk ⌧ 26 & 30 Berwick St W1 ⏱ 10am-8pm Mon-Fri, 10am-7pm Sat-Sun ⊖ Oxford Circus/ Piccadilly Circus

Rough Trade (2, B3)
With its underground, alternative and vintage rarities, this home of the eponymous punk-music label remains a haven for

Vinyl junkie on the loose

vinyl junkies who get misty-eyed about the days before CDs (also sold here) and even, heavens, before the Apple iPod.
☎ 7229 8541
🖥 www.roughtrade.com
✉ 130 Talbot Rd W11
🕙 10am-6.30pm Mon-Sat, 1pm-5pm Sun
⊖ Ladbroke Grove/ Westbourne Park

Sister Ray (6, C2)
If you're the type to listen to the venerable John Peel on the BBC/BBC World Service, this specialist in innovative, experimental and indie music will rock your world.
☎ 7287 8385 ✉ 94 Berwick St W1 🕙 10am-8pm Mon-Fri, 10am-7pm Sat & Sun ⊖ Oxford Circus/Piccadilly Circus

BOOKS

The capital of a still very literary-minded nation, whatever the accusations of dumbing-down, London is a good place to fossick for a wide range of reasonably priced books. True, chains have given the trade more of an assembly-line feel, but eminently browsable specialist stores remain.

Books for Cooks (2, B3)
Like what you've read in this emporium of gastro-porn (ie cookery books)? Then sample some of the recipes in the small café attached.
☎ 7221 1992 🖥 www.booksforcooks.com ✉ 4 Blenheim Crescent W11
🕙 10am-6pm Mon-Sat
⊖ Ladbroke Grove

Forbidden Planet (6, D2)
A treasure-trove of comics, sci-fi, horror and fantasy literature, Forbidden Planet

must have surely benefited from the global success of *Lord of the Rings*. It moved into these shiny new premises in 2003.
☎ 7836 4179 🖥 www.forbiddenplanet.com ✉ 179 Shaftesbury Ave 🕙 10am-7pm Mon-Sat, to 8pm Thu, noon-6pm Sun ⊖ Leicester Sq/ Covent Garden

Foyles (6, D1)
Thankfully it no longer arranges books by publisher,

and its old-fashioned chit system of purchase is a memory, but this now sensibly organised independent bookstore still prides itself on the breadth of its range. Women's book specialist Silver Moon, music store Ray's Jazz, and a café are found under its roof.
☎ 7437 5660 🖥 www.foyles.co.uk ✉ 113-119 Charing Cross Rd WC2
🕙 9.30am-7.30pm Mon-Sat, noon-6pm Sun ⊖ Tottenham Court Rd

The Word on London

Ever since the *Canterbury Tales*, in which Chaucer's pilgrims gathered for their trip at the Tabard Inn in Southwark, London has provided a literary backdrop. Daniel Defoe chronicled the plague year of 1665, *Samuel Pepys' Diary* includes a description of the Great Fire a year later, and Charles Dickens' name still evokes the squalor and poverty of working-class Victorian London – think *Oliver Twist*.

More contemporary tales include Graham Greene's *The End of the Affair*, set in Clapham Common during WWI; Michael Moorcock's *Mother London*, an engaging history of the city from the Blitz to the '80s as told by three mental hospital outpatients; and Martin Amis' *London Fields*, a dire but gripping portrait of London lowlife.

Timothy Mo's humorous *Sour Sweet*, about a Chinese family in London, gives an immigrant's perspective, as do other prominent writers such as Zadie Smith (see p107).

Gay's the Word (3, D2)
For more than 25 years now, Gay has been the word in everything from advice books on coming out to queer and lesbian literature.
☎ 7278 7654 🖳 www
.gaystheword.co.uk
✉ 66 Marchmont St
WC1 🕒 10am-6.30pm
Mon-Sat, 2-6pm Sun
⊖ Russell Sq

Grant & Cutler (6, B2)
This is London's best foreign-language bookshop, whether you're taking your first steps in Spanish, want a dictionary to translate from your own language to English or are a postgraduate student of Chekhov.
☎ 7734 2012 🖳 www
.grantandcutler.com
✉ 55-57 Great Marlborough St W1 🕒 9am-6pm
Mon-Sat, to 7pm Thu
⊖ Oxford Circus

Helter Skelter (6, D1)
Literate rock fans will be enthralled by this store, which stocks everything from in-depth band biographies to fanzines.
☎ 7836 1151 🖳 www
.helterskelterbooks.com
✉ 4 Denmark St WC2
🕒 10am-7pm Mon-Fri, 10am-6pm Sat ⊖ Tottenham Court Rd

Magma Books (3, D2)
Magma explodes with books, magazines and more on cool, cutting-edge design. There's also a smaller branch in Covent Garden (6, D2 ☎ 7240 8498; 8 Earlham St ⊖ Leicester Sq).
☎ 7242 9503 🖳 www
.magmabooks.com
✉ 117-119 Clerkenwell

Book Chains
Waterstone's, the home-grown answer to the American chain Borders, seems warmer and more personable than its transatlantic rival, but maybe that's just us. Books etc is part of Borders. Blackwells is an academic publisher that's crossed over into general bookselling. Besides the major outlets below, you'll find branches across town.
- **Blackwell's** (6, D2 ☎ 7292 5100; www .blackwells.co.uk; 100 Charing Cross Rd WC2 ⊖ Tottenham Court Rd)
- **Books etc** (6, E2 ☎ 7379 6947; www.borders .co.uk; 26 James St WC2 ⊖ Covent Garden)
- **Borders** (6, A1 ☎ 7292 1600; www.borders .co.uk; 203 Oxford St W1 ⊖ Oxford Circus)
- **Waterstone's** (6, B4 ☎ 7851 2400; www .waterstones.co.uk; 203-206 Piccadilly W1 ⊖ Piccadilly Circus)

Rd EC1 🕒 10am-7pm Mon-Sat, to 8pm Thu, noon-6pm Sun
⊖ Farringdon

Murder One (6, D2)
Hard-boiled crime fiction from the likes of Carl Hiaasen, Elmore Leonard, Walter Mosley and Sara Paretsky sit spine-to-spine with sci-fi drama and pulp romances in this cult shop.
☎ 7734 3485 ✉ 71-73 Charing Cross Rd WC2
🕒 10am-7pm Mon-Wed, 10am-8pm Thu-Sat

⊖ Tottenham Court Rd/Leicester Sq

Sportspages (6, D2)
Get the inside track on sporting heroes, from *Wisden Cricketers' Almanack* and contemporary biographies to witty exposés of 1970s Scottish footballers' shenanigans.
☎ 7240 9604 🖳 www
.sportsbooksdirect.co.uk
✉ 94-96 Charing Cross Rd WC2 🕒 9.30am-7pm Mon-Sat, noon-6pm Sun ⊖ Leicester Sq/Tottenham Court Rd

Stanfords (6, D2)
As a 150-year-old seller of maps, guides and literature, the granddaddy of travel bookstores is a destination in its own right. Ernest Shackleton, David Livingstone, Michael Palin and Brad Pitt have all been customers.
☎ 7836 1321
🖥 www.stanfords.co.uk
✉ 12-14 Long Acre WC2
🕙 9am-7.30pm Mon-Fri, from 9.30am Tue, 10am-7pm Sat, noon-6pm Sun
🚇 Covent Garden

The Travel Bookshop (2, B3)
Hugh Grant's shop in the movie *Notting Hill* was closely modelled on this one. Alongside the latest guidebooks, you'll find travel literature plus out-of-print and antiquarian gems.
☎ 7229 5260 🖥 www .thetravelbookshop.co.uk
✉ 13 Blenheim Crescent W11 🕙 10am-6pm Mon-Sat, 11am-4pm Sun
🚇 Ladbroke Grove

Zwemmer Art & Architecture (6, D2)
With one of Zwemmer's covetable fine-art tomes on your coffee table, you'll never forget your London trip. The branch (6, B6) opposite at 80 Charing Cross Rd specialises in books on photography and cinema.
☎ 7240 4158
🖥 www.zwemmer.com
✉ 24 Litchfield St WC2
🕙 10am-6.30pm Mon-Fri, to 8pm Thu, 10am-6pm Sat
🚇 Tottenham Court Rd

FOOD & DRINK

Don't forget the food halls at Harrods, Selfridges and Fortnum & Mason. If you want to be a favoured party guest, take along a cake from Patisserie Valerie or Maison Bertaux (see p77).

Algerian Coffee Stores (6, C2)
Wonderful aromas assail the senses when you enter this store, which sells flavoured coffees and teas like vanilla and orange.
☎ 7437 2480 🖥 www .algcoffee.co.uk ✉ 52 Old Compton St W1 🕙 9am-7pm Mon-Sat 🚇 Leicester Sq/Piccadilly Circus

Neal's Yard Dairy (6, D2)
Proving that the English can hold their own (nose) when it comes to ripe, smelly cheeses, this shops stocks more than 70 varieties,

including specialist farmhouse cheeses.
☎ 7240 5700 ✉ 17 Shorts Gardens WC2
🕙 9am-7pm Mon-Sat
🚇 Covent Garden

Rococo (2, D5)
This legendary, and legendarily expensive, chocolate shop is an unforgettable treat for those with a sweet tooth. Try the Belgian Godiva or French Valrhona cooking chocolate.
☎ 7352 5857
🖥 www.rococochocol ates.com ✉ 321 King's Rd SW3 🕙 9.30am-6pm

Mon-Fri, 9.30am-5pm Sat
🚇 Sloane Sq

The Tea House (6, E2)
For evidence that the English acquired their famous taste for tea from other cultures, check out the varieties and accoutrements (eg ornate Chinese tea cups) here.
☎ 7240 7539 ✉ 15a Neal St WC2 🕙 10am-7pm Mon-Sat, noon-6pm Sun 🚇 Covent Garden

The Vintage House (6, C2)
There are some dusty bottles of vintage grape here, but the main attraction is the array of single-malt Scotch whiskies, from peaty Lagavulin to the smooth MacCallan.
☎ 7437 5112 🖥 www .sohowhisky.com ✉ 42 Old Compton Rd W1
🕙 9am-11pm Mon-Fri, 9.30am-11pm Sat, noon-11pm Sun 🚇 Leicester Sq/Tottenham Court Rd

---

Supermarket Sweep
For self-caterers or picnickers, two central supermarkets are **Sainsbury's** (3, C3 ☎ 7580 7820; 15-17 Tottenham Court Rd W1 🚇 Tottenham Court Rd) and **Tesco Metro** (6, E3 ☎ 7853 7500; 21 Bedford St WC2 🚇 Covent Garden/Leicester Sq). Both chains have outlets throughout town.

FOR CHILDREN

Benjamin Pollock's Toy Shop (6, D2)
You know the saying 'they don't make them like they used to'? Well, they do here in this charming and cluttered little cavern of hand-crafted toys.
☎ 7379 7866 ▢ www.pollocks-coventgarden.co.uk ✉ 44 The Market, Covent Garden WC2 ⏱ 10.30am-6pm Mon-Sat, noon-5pm Sun ⊖ Covent Garden

Children's Book Centre (2, B5)
This is a wonderful shop for children with standard books as well as the talking variety, videos, CDs, toys, chocolates and even jewellery.
☎ 7937 7497 ▢ www.childrensbookcentre.co.uk ✉ 237 Kensington High St W8 ⏱ 9.30am-6.30pm Mon-Sat, to 6pm

Tue, to 7pm Thu, noon-6pm Sun ⊖ High St Kensington

Compendia (5, A2)
This shop is piled high with board and other games, including a good selection of travel-themed ones.
☎ 8293 6616 ✉ 10 The Market, Greenwich SE10 ⏱ noon-5.30pm Mon-Fri, 10.30am-5.30pm Sat-Sun 🚉 DLR Cutty Sark

Daisy & Tom (2, D5)
Gorgeous (and pricey) kids' clothes, shoes and toys are available here, with a marionette show, carousel rides and even haircuts to keep the kids occupied.
☎ 7352 5000 ✉ 181-183 King's Rd SW3 ⏱ 10am-6pm Mon-Fri, to 7pm Wed, 10am-6.30pm Sat, noon-6pm Sun ⊖ Sloane Sq

Hamleys (6, A2)
London's most famous toy store doesn't disappoint. It's an Aladdin's cave of playthings, with traditional board games, computer games, cowboy hats, teddy bears and everything in between.
☎ 7494 2000 ▢ www.hamleys.com ✉ 188-196 Regent St W1 ⏱ 10am-8pm Mon-Fri, 9.30am-8pm Sat, noon-6pm Sun ⊖ Oxford Circus

Kite Store (6, E2)
This shop stocks at least 100 different models as well as Frisbees, boomerangs and other things that go whirr in the sky.
☎ 7836 1666 ✉ 48 Neal St WC2 ⏱ 10am-6pm Mon-Fri, 10.30am-6pm Sat ⊖ Covent Garden

SPECIALIST STORES

Inflate (3, F2)
As the name suggests, nearly everything in this small boutique is inflatable, from the egg cup and postcard to the comfy armchair. Genius.
☎ 7713 9096 ▢ www.inflate.co.uk ✉ 28 Exmouth Market EC1 ⏱ 9.30am-6pm Mon-Fri ⊖ Farringdon

Mathmos (6, D2)
The lava lamp, one of the great British icons of the 1960s, continues to bubble away here. The damned things are so mesmerising, though, it's difficult to choose just one.
☎ 7836 8587 ✉ 8 Shorts Gardens WC2 ⏱ 10.30am-7.30pm

Mon-Sat, 11.30am-5pm Sun ⊖ Covent Garden

A rather light-headed David

Not Shopped Out Yet?
If you've still got presents to buy and your credit card is holding up, make your next purchase the annual *Time Out Shopping Guide* (£6.99), with details of nearly every retail outlet in town.

Eating

The politically correct term would be something like 'culinarily challenged', but however you describe it London has traditionally limped behind other world capitals in the matter of food.

No longer – thank goodness. London's restaurants have finally come of age, egged on by a population who saw what the rest of the world had to offer, a phalanx of celebrity TV chefs such as Jamie Oliver and Nigella Lawson, and, ahem, an influx of Australasian cooks.

Today, the international cognoscenti rate several London restaurants – among them Gordon Ramsay, Nahm, Hakkasan and

The Cost of a Meal

Our pricing symbols represent the cost per person for dinner and generally includes two courses and a drink. Count on paying less for lunch.

£	Under £15
££	£15 to £25
£££	£25 to £40
££££	Over £40

the quirky Les Trois Garçons – as places to dine before you die. Ordinary fans of Mr Oliver's ignore mixed reviews and book months ahead for Fifteen, while restaurateurs further down the food chain have had to add spice to appease increasingly fussy customers.

Simply irresistible Souvlaki & Bar (p66)

The city's cosmopolitan make-up means a diverse range of cuisines, from the ubiquitous Indian to the rarer Eritrean, and even British staples such as sausages and mash, have been given a makeover by a nouveau generation of chefs.

All this said, however, you just don't get the same value for money as in other foodie destinations such as San Francisco or Sydney. While you can enjoy a fantastic curry for less than a tenner, it's still easy to lose £30 on an indifferent meal. So it pays to peruse listings carefully.

London's gastronomy, which still doesn't do decent Vietnamese, for example, hasn't quite reached the heady heights that locals believe – it's just 10 times better than it used to be. And we don't have the heart to tell them they were the last to join the revolution.

Booking Tables

Making a reservation is just about compulsory for all central restaurants from Thursday to Saturday and for the hippest ones at all times. Internet booking service www.toptable.co.uk is reliable and offers discounts. Many top restaurants operate a system of multiple seatings, say from 7pm to 9pm and 9pm to 11pm. Given a choice, go for the later seating, when you won't be rushed.

BLOOMSBURY & CLERKENWELL

Abeno (3, D3) ££
Japanese
This understated little restaurant specialises in *okonomi-yaki*, a kind of Japanese omelette that is combined with your ingredients of choice and cooked at the table.
☎ 7405 3211 ✉ 47 Museum St WC1 ☺ noon-10pm ⊖ Tottenham Court Rd ♿

Club Gascon (3, G3) ££££
French
Instead of enjoying just one main course at this formal Michelin-starred restaurant, you select four or five tapas-style portions. Exquisite duck, squid, cassoulet and plenty of foie gras all feature.
☎ 7796 0600 ✉ 57 West Smithfield EC1 ☺ noon-2pm & 7-11pm Mon-Fri, 7-11pm Sat ⊖ Farringdon/Barbican

Le Café du Marché (3, G2) £££
French
Tradition is a watchword in the exposed brick warehouse of this rustic French restaurant – think hearty dishes with garlic and rosemary flavours. There's often live jazz and piano upstairs.
☎ 7608 1609 ✉ 22 Charterhouse Sq, Charterhouse Mews EC1 ☺ noon-2.30pm & 6-10pm Mon-Fri, 6-10pm Sat ⊖ Farringdon

Hakkasan (6, C1) £££
Chinese
This tucked-away basement restaurant's low ultra-violet lighting and swanky cocktail bar have made it a hit with the in set. Delicious dim sum and artfully presented Chinese dishes have won it a Michelin star. Hakkasan is – deservedly – one of London's hottest meal tickets. Despite reports of haughty service, lunchtime staff are charm itself.
☎ 7907 1888 ✉ 8 Hanway Place WC2 ☺ noon-midnight Mon-Tue, to 2am Wed-Sat, to 11.30pm Sun ⊖ Tottenham Court Rd Ⓥ

Little Bay (3, F2) £
International
Kitsch Little Bay is memorable not only for its gargoyles and DIY chandeliers (made from stripped electrical wire and marbles);

Squeeze in more at Moro

it also serves good-quality meals at bargain prices. Its amazing Egyptian-themed sister, LMNT (2, H1 ☎ 7249 6727; 316 Queensbridge Rd E8 ⓇLondon Fields) is in Hackney.
☎ 7278 1234 ✉ 171 Farringdon Rd EC1 ☺ 8.30am-midnight ⊖ Farringdon ♿ Ⓥ

Moro (3, F2) £££
Middle Eastern
North African, Spanish and Portuguese fusion cuisine as featured in the famous Moro cookbooks is served up in a buzzy, souk-like environment.
☎ 7833 8336 ✉ 34-36 Exmouth Market N1 ☺ 12.30-2.30pm & 7-10.30pm ⊖ Farringdon

North Sea Fish Restaurant (3, D1) ££
Seafood
The deep-fried or grilled cod, haddock and plaice are a cut above the norm here and always served with a huge helping of chips.
☎ 7387 5892 ✉ 7-8 Leigh St WC1 ☺ noon-2.30pm Mon-Sat, 5.30-10.30pm Sun ⊖ Russell Sq ♿

JONATHAN SMITH

Tipping
London waiters aren't like New Yorkers: they won't chase you down the street if you don't leave a tip. But they aren't paid handsomely, so failing to leave 10% to 15% extra is tantamount to saying the service was unsatisfactory. Recently, restaurants have started adding a discretionary service charge (around 12.5%) to the bill, so be careful not to pay twice. You can ask your waiter whether the service charge is given to them. If not, don't pay it and hand over your tip direct.

St John (3, G2) £££
British
This restaurant for carnivores serves parts of an animal that others do not reach. Excellent Olde English cuisine dished up in its minimalist white dining room includes calf's liver, bone-marrow salad, ox tongue and pig's spleen.

Oh, yeah, there are some lentils on the menu.
☎ 7251 0848 ✉ 26 St John St EC1 ☉ noon-3pm & 6-11pm Mon-Fri, 6-11pm Sat ⊖ Farringdon

Souvlaki & Bar (3, F2) ££
Greek
Greek tapas and pork or lamb souvlaki make a tasty light lunch or dinner. This attractive bar-restaurant, with its horseshoe-shaped lights, is an offshoot of the laudable Real Greek (3, H1 ☎ 7739 8212; 15 Hoxton Market N1 ⊖ Old St).
☎ 7253 7234 ✉ 142 St John St EC1 ☉ 10am-11pm Mon-Sat ⊖ Farringdon Ⓥ

CAMDEN & HAMPSTEAD

Cotton's Rhum Shop, Bar & Restaurant (4, B2) ££
Caribbean
Whether you fall into the camp of those who prefer this to the Mango Room (see below), or vice versa, there's no denying they're worthy rivals. The curried goat here is particularly good.
☎ 7485 8388 ✉ 55 Chalk Farm Rd NW1 ☉ 5pm-midnight Mon-Thu, 11am-midnight Fri-Sun ⊖ Chalk Farm

The Engineer (4, A2) ££
Pub Grub
This pretty Victorian conversion attracts a groovy north London set. It tends towards the formal and starch end of the gastropub range.
☎ 7722 0950 ✉ 65 Gloucester Ave NW1 ☉ 9am-11pm Mon-Sat, 9am-10.30pm Sun ⊖ Chalk Farm

The eminent Engineer

Galangal (4, B3) ££
Thai
The curries, noodles and soups at this funky, slightly retro-style canteen leave you feeling healthy and uplifted. (Perhaps that's just the apple and ginger juice talking!)
☎ 7483 3765 ✉ 29-31 Parkway NW1 ☉ noon-3pm & 6-11pm Mon-Fri, 1.30-11.30pm Sat, 1-10.30pm Sun ⊖ Camden Town

Jin Kichi (2, C1) £££
Japanese
Simply put, when so many Japanese customers favour this restaurant, despite its shabby appearance, you know it must be good. Book, and then go for the grills.
☎ 7794 6158 ✉ 73 Heath St NW3 ☉ 6-11pm Tue-Fri, 12.30-2pm & 6-11pm Sat & Sun ⊖ Hampstead

Mango Room (4, C2) ££/£££
Caribbean
Behind the aqua-blue façade on the littered street lies a restaurant that's vibrant in both décor and atmosphere. A perfect meal here? Try a saltfish and ackee starter, goat curry, and then a mango and banana *brûlée*.
☎ 7482 5065 ✉ 10 Kentish Town Rd NW1 ☉ noon-3pm & 6pm-midnight Tue-Sun, 6pm-midnight Sun ⊖ Camden Town

Odette's (4, A2) £££
French
Its opulent velvet décor and gilt mirrors make Odette's perfect for a romantic dinner. Though the food is theoretically French (and the excellent wines still are), an Italian influence is creeping in.
☎ 7586 5486 ✉ 130 Regent's Park Rd NW1 ☉ 12.30-2.30pm & 7-11pm Mon-Fri, 7-11pm Sat, 12.30-2.30pm Sun ⊖ Chalk Farm

Trojka (4, A2) ££
Eastern European
Take a seat in this attractive, sky-lit restaurant for borscht and rye bread, herrings with dill sauce, Polish *bigosz* (cabbage stew with meats) and other Eastern European specialities.
☎ 7483 3765 ✉ 101 Regents Park Rd NW1 ☉ noon-10.30pm ⊖ Chalk Farm

CENTRAL LONDON

Café in the Crypt (6, D4) £
International
Extremely central and set beneath St Martin-in-the-Fields, the atmospheric crypt café (complete with gravestones) is one of those essential tourist destinations that many race to in their time in London, but then rarely set foot in again. It serves salads, quiches and other good, solid food.
☎ 7839 4342 ✉ St Martin-in-the-Fields, Duncannon St WC2 🕒 8am-10pm Mon-Wed, 10am-11pm Thu-Sat, noon-8pm Sun ⊖ Charing Cross ♿ Ⓥ

Café Lazeez Soho (6, C2) ££
Indian
When you're tired of waiting for a table in this busy area or want to avoid the din a bit, come to the branch of this nouveau Indian chain that's located in the Soho Theatre. It serves fresh and delicious food.
☎ 7434 9393 ✉ 21 Dean St W1 🕒 11am-midnight Mon-Sat ⊖ Tottenham Court Rd Ⓥ

Criterion (6, C3) £££
French
This place on Piccadilly Circus has a spectacular interior that one breathless critic has compared to the inside of a Fabergé egg. The menu offers fashionable modern French food, plus some English classics such as fish and chips.
☎ 7930 0488 ✉ 224 Piccadilly W1 🕒 noon-2.30pm & 5.30-11.30pm Mon-Sat, 5.30-10.30pm Sun ⊖ Piccadilly Circus

East@West (6, D2) ££££
Asian
Tatler magazine's best new restaurant of the year 2004 serves small, tapas-style portions, allowing you to sample its panoply of pan-Asian flavours, peppered with European and American tones. Celebrity Aussie chef Christine Manfield runs the kitchen.
☎ 7010 8600 ✉ 13-15 West St WC2 🕒 noon-3pm & 5.30pm-midnight Mon-Fri, 5.30pm-midnight Sat ⊖ Leicester Sq

Gaby's (6, D3) £
Turkish
Halfway between a kebab shop *par excellence* and a New York deli, this tiny Soho stalwart serves much tastier falafel, couscous, pastrami, baklava etc than its strip-lighting, laminated menus and Formica tables would suggest.
☎ 7836 4233 ✉ 30 Charing Cross Rd WC1

Café in the Crypt: to die for

🕒 9am-midnight Mon-Sat, 11am-midnight Sun ⊖ Leicester Sq ♿ Ⓥ

Gay Hussar (6, C1) £££
Hungarian
The dark-wood panelled dining room is pure old-school Soho of the 1950s, even if the caricatures on the walls by *Guardian* newspaper cartoonist Martin Rowson are much more contemporary. Traditional Hungarian dishes come in huge portions.
☎ 7437 0973 ✉ 2 Greek St W1 🕒 12.15-2.30pm & 5.30-10.45pm Mon-Sat ⊖ Tottenham Court Rd

---

Currying Favour
Even at its culinary worst, London was always one of the world capitals of curry. The traditional destination was **Brick Lane** (3, J2 ⊖ Liverpool St). But many of the curry houses, mostly Bengali, now lining that street are overpriced and overrated, so those in the know head south for the exciting mix of subcontinental cuisines along **Tooting Broadway** and **Tooting High St** (2, F6 ⊖ Tooting Broadway). The more central **Drummond St** (3, C2 ⊖ Warren St/Euston Sq) also has a small cluster of decent *bhel poori* houses, serving mild south Indian cuisine.

The Ivy (6, D2) £££
Modern British
If you're not one of the numerous celebrity clientele continually ambushed by the paparazzi outside the Ivy, it can be difficult to get a table. The restaurant has long been a favourite of one Mrs V Beckham. (So, we envious types ask, couldn't they fatten her up a bit?)
☎ 7836 4751 ✉ 1 West St WC2 🕑 noon-3pm & 5.30pm-midnight Mon-Sat, noon-3.30pm & 5pm-midnight Sun ⊖ Leicester Sq

J Sheekey (6, D3) £££
Seafood
This sister to the Ivy is easier to book. In its four interconnected dining rooms, you'll find fresh fish, shrimps, fish cakes, caviar, lobster, crab hummus and even a few veggie options.
☎ 7240 2565 ✉ 28-32 St Martin's Ct WC2 🕑 noon-3pm & 5pm-midnight ⊖ Leicester Sq

Kettners (6, D2) ££
Italian
There can't be many places serving champagne with pizza (or burgers), but this upmarket Pizza Express offshoot does exactly that. Naturally, the fare is slightly higher quality than the norm, enjoyed against a backdrop of tinkly piano music.
☎ 7734 6112 ✉ 29 Romilly St W1 🕑 noon-midnight ⊖ Leicester Sq ♿ Ⓥ

Lindsay House (6, C2) ££££
British
Atmospheric, 18th-century Lindsay House stills feel like a private home and you have to ring the bell to gain admission. Irish chef Richard Corrigan produces big, bold flavours, for which he's won a Michelin star. No prizes for the high-handed service, though.
☎ 7439 0450 ✉ 21 Romilly St W1 🕑 noon-2.30pm & 6-11pm Mon-Fri, 6-11pm Sat ⊖ Leicester Sq

Mezzo (6, C2) £££
European
While many Londoners have generally lost their taste for huge, Terence Conran–run eateries – observe the past-it status of the Atlantic Bar &

Mezzo: nothing by halves

Grill and Quaglino's – Mezzo's location in the heart of media land seems to have kept it buzzing. The cheaper and more casual Mezzonine is on the ground floor.
☎ 7314 4000 ✉ 100 Wardour St W1 🕑 6pm-12.30am Mon-Thu, 6pm-2.30am Fri-Sat, 6-10.30pm Sun ⊖ Piccadilly Circus Ⓥ

Mildred's (6, B2) ££
Vegetarian
Formerly the archetypal alternative-lifestyle caff, Mildred's has spread its wings in spacious new premises. Wholesome and tasty are the best words to describe

---

Veggie Victuals

The country that – years ago – gave the world The Smiths and the song 'Meat is Murder' just wouldn't get away with being unfriendly to vegetarians. Many Asian Britons shun meat for religious reasons and you can eat your fill of vegetables in the capital's curry houses (see p67). But most ordinary restaurants also offer at least a few veggie choices (and those marked Ⓥ offer a lot). Excellent exclusively vegetarian outlets include the Gate (see p68), Mildred's (pictured, see above) and Food for Thought (see p74).

the salads, stir-fries, veggie burgers and pies, which still keep the place packed.
☎ 7494 1634 ✉ 45 Lexington St W1 ◷ noon-11pm Mon-Sat ⊖ Piccadilly Circus/Tottenham Court Rd ♿ Ⓥ

Momo (6, A3) £££
Middle Eastern
The kasbah comes to London at this trendy Moroccan restaurant, with excellent couscous and *tajines*. Mo, the attached 'salad bar, tearoom and bazaar', is cheaper, though the service often leaves something to be desired.
☎ 7434 4040 ✉ 25 Heddon St W1 ◷ noon-2.30pm & 7-11pm ⊖ Piccadilly Circus ♿ Ⓥ

Providores (3, A3) ££
Fusion
Some contend that Kiwi Peter Gordon is the only chef in London who should be trusted with fusion cuisine. Here, he's moved from his earlier Pacific Rim to Spanish and Mediterranean mixtures, but with equally lip-smacking results. The ground-floor Tapa Room is cheaper and more casual.
☎ 7935 6175 ✉ 109 Marylebone High St W1 ◷ 9-11.30am Mon-Fri, noon-3pm & 6-10.30pm Sat & Sun ⊖ Baker St ♿ Ⓥ

Quo Vadis (6, C2) £
Italian
Karl Marx's one-time home is now an elegant, formal dining room, with stained glass and medically themed art. Executive chef Marco Pierre White oversees the menu, which includes classics such as veal and wild mushrooms.
☎ 7437 9585 ✉ 26-29 Dean St W1 ◷ noon-3pm & 5.30-11.30pm Mon-Fri, 5.30-11.30pm Sat ⊖ Tottenham Court Rd

Rainforest Café (6, C3) £/££
One for the kids, this café has animatronic birds and beasts roaring and hooting in a 'jungle', while burgers, Tex-Mex and Caribbean food is served out.
☎ 7434 3111 ✉ 20 Shaftesbury Ave W1 ◷ noon-10pm Mon-Fri, noon-8pm Sat, 11.30am-10pm Sun ⊖ Piccadilly Circus ♿ Ⓥ

Rock & Sole Plaice (6, E1) ££
British
The basic Formica tables upstairs are no-nonsense, but the fish and chips are fancier; alongside the old favourite (and increasingly rare) cod, you can choose dover sole, scotch salmon or tuna steak in batter.
☎ 7836 3785 ✉ 47 Endell St WC2 ◷ 11.30am-10pm Mon-Sat, noon-9pm Sun ⊖ Covent Garden ♿

Simpson's-in-the-Strand (6, F3) ££
British
Roasts and joints of meat are wheeled to your table on a silver trolley in this traditional, if stuffy, panelled dining room.
☎ 7836 9112 ✉ 100 Strand WC2 ◷ 11.30am-10pm Mon-Sat, noon-9pm Sun ⊖ Covent Garden/Charing Cross

Sketch (6, A2) ££££££
International
Toilet cubicles shaped like eggs, a video wall, blow-up furniture and generally stunning design make Sketch a hot ticket, but à la *Spinal Tap*, the bills go to 11 here. Upstairs in the opulent Lecture Room, the food often seems worth the outrageous cost (£65 for a starter!); downstairs in the minimalist gallery you might resent £50 all in.
☎ 0870 777 4488 ✉ 9 Conduit St W1 ◷ noon-2pm & 7-10.30pm Tue-Sat ⊖ Oxford Circus

Souk (6, C1) ££
Middle Eastern
With its hookahs and Persian carpets, it's tempting to call this the poor man's Momo. The thing is, though,

Stunning food, stunning design, stunning cost – Sketch

that its friendly, unpretentious vibe, reasonably priced *tajines* and occasional live music often make Souk seem the real winner. ☎ 7240 1796 ✉ 27 Litchfield St WC2 ✪ noon-11.30pm ⊖ Leicester Sq/Tottenham Court Rd

Villandry (3, B2) £££
Mediterranean
This is essentially a delicatessen with a simple and stylish dining room attached. Dishes to try include rustic white-bean stew flavoured with shavings of black truffle, but it's best to choose the simplest dishes – and then finish with the celebrated cheese platter. ☎ 7631 3131 ✉ 170 Great Portland St W1 ✪ 8am-11pm Mon-Sat, 11am-4pm Sun ⊖ Great Portland St

CHELSEA & BELGRAVIA

Gordon Ramsay (2, D6) ££££
European
The only London restaurant with three Michelin stars is run by *the* flag-bearer for new British cooking. Say what you like about Ramsay's temperament, everything that's served here – from pigeon and venison to foie gras and truffles – attests to his enormous talent. ☎ 7352 4441 ✉ 68-69 Royal Hospital Rd SW3

JONATHAN SMITH
Gordon Ramsay savoir-faire

✪ noon-2.30pm & 6.30-11pm Mon-Fri ⊖ Sloane Sq

Poule au Pot (2, D5) £££
French
This country-style French restaurant is considered by many as the best in London. Admittedly, it's not the best value, but it's the romantic, candle-lit ambience you're paying for. There's also an alfresco terrace that's lovely in the warmer months. ☎ 7730 7763 ✉ 231 Ebury St SW1 ✪ 12.30-2.30pm & 7-11.15pm Mon-Sat, to 10.30pm Sun ⊖ Sloane Sq ⚹

EAST END & THE CITY

Arkansas Café (3, J1) ££
American
Good ole down-home country cookin' is served up in this unit on the edge of Spitalfields market (and reached via the inside of the market). Its ribs, corn-fed chicken and steak are popular with City workers. ☎ 7377 6999 ✉ Unit 12, Spitalfields Market, 107b Commercial St E1 ✪ noon-2.30pm Mon-Fri, noon-4pm Sun ⊖ Liverpool St/Aldgate East

Armadillo (2, H2) ££
Latin American
A simple neighbourhood restaurant that some people travel across London to visit, Armadillo has a constantly changing menu of excellent Argentinian, Brazilian and Peruvian food, and sparse touches of Latino kitsch (eg beaded curtains with pictures of Jesus and Frida Kahlo). ☎ 7249 3633 ✉ 41 Broadway Market E8 ✪ 6.30-10.30pm ⊞ London Fields or ⊟ 106, 253, 26, 48, 55

Café Spice Namaste (3, J4) £££
Indian
Inside this old magistrates' court, now spiced up in bright Oriental colours, you'll find excellent Parsee/Goan cuisine, including a famous *dhansak* (lamb or vegetable stew with rice, lentils and vegetables). Although off the beaten track, it's only 10 minutes from Tower Hill. ☎ 7488 9242 ✉ 16 Prescot St E1 ✪ noon-3pm & 6.30-10.30pm Mon-Fri, 6.30-10.30pm Sat ⊖ Tower Hill Ⓥ

Eyre Brothers (3, H2) ££££
Spanish/African
Geographically located in Shoreditch, but stylistically

with one foot in the City, this dark-panelled, low-ceilinged den attracts slightly older diners with its interesting range of Spanish/Portuguese/Mozambiquean food.
☎ 7613 5346 ✉ 70 Leonard St EC2 🕒 noon-3pm & 6.30-10.45pm Mon-Fri, 6.30-10.45pm Sat ⊖ Old St

Fifteen (3, H1)   ££££
British/Mediterranean
Jamie Oliver's gaff – a not-for-profit venture to train 15 young homeless people as chefs – is as bright and breezy as the cheeky chappie himself. Getting a table, however, is no laughing matter. You can walk into the deli bar (🕒 8am-11pm

Business Affair
For the right place to mix business and the pleasure of dining, try:
- Club Gascon   (p65)
- Eyre Brothers (p70)
- St John   (p66)
- Moro   (p65)
- Café Spice Namaste   (p70)
- Oxo Tower   (p75)
- Les Trois Garçons   (above)

Mon-Fri, 8am-5pm Sun), otherwise ring m-o-n-t-h-s ahead.
☎ 7251 1515 ✉ 15 Westland Place N1 🕒 booking line 9.30am-5.30pm Mon-Fri, restaurant noon-3pm & 7-10pm Mon-Fri, 7-10pm Sat, 8am-5pm Sun ⊖ Old St ♿ Ⓥ

Les Trois Garçons (3, J2)   ££££
French
What's the French for va-va-voom? Perhaps the answer is this over-the-top converted pub, where the deer heads, stuffed giraffe and taxidermied crocodile all wear diamond necklaces and tiaras, while handbags and long strings of diamantes hang from the ceiling. The modern cuisine (Gallic-inspired, of course) has improved, and there's a good-value set menu Monday to Wednesday.
☎ 7613 1924 ✉ 1 Club Row E1 🕒 7-10pm Mon-Sat ⊖ Liverpool St

New Tayyab (2, H3)   £
Indian
The enticing aroma you smell on entering is Punjabi cuisine, such as *seekh* (shish) kebabs, *masala* fish and *karahi* wok dishes,

Les Trois Garçons: simply divine, dahling

being readied and served. Vegetarian dishes are offered, but it's carnivores who will leave happiest.
☎ 7247 9543 ✉ 83 Fieldgate St E1 🕒 5pm-midnight ⊖ Whitechapel Ⓥ

Ye Olde Cheshire Cheese (3, F3)   £££
British
For the times you just want to play the tourist, this low-lit, 17th-century pub has a traditional chop room. Past customers include Mark Twain, Charles Dickens and Samuel Johnson.
☎ 7353 6170 ✉ Wine Office Court, off Fleet St EC4 🕒 noon-9pm Mon-Sat, noon-2.30pm Sun ⊖ Blackfriars ♿ Ⓥ

ISLINGTON

Almeida (2, F1)   £££
French
One of the newer and better outlets run by the prolific restaurateur Terence Conran, Almeida's decent-sized dining room serves classic French dishes that are reliably good – and the

accommodating staff are more than willing to help translate the French-language menu.
☎ 7354 4777 ✉ 30 Almeida St N1 🕒 noon-3pm & 6.30-11pm, to 10.30pm Sun ⊖ Angel/Highbury & Islington

Gallipoli (2, F2)   £
Turkish
The best budget option along Upper St, and not bad for those with cash to burn, Gallipoli is a crammed cheek-by-jowl place with funky Turkish decoration. If you can't get in for

moussaka, hummus and other delicious dishes here, there's Gallipoli Again, at 120 Upper St.
☎ 7359 0630 ✉ 102 Upper St N1 ☽ 10.30am-11pm, to midnight Fri-Sat ⊖ Angel/Highbury & Islington

Giraffe (2, F2)　£/££
International
Despite the potential pitfalls of being a chain outlet always jam-packed with middle-class young families, brightly coloured Giraffe manages to win over nearly everyone with

Turkish fare and flair at Gallipoli

Stand-out choice, Giraffe

its fresh, healthy food and upbeat atmosphere.
☎ 7359 5999 ✉ 29-31 Essex Rd N1 ☽ 8am-11.30pm Mon-Fri, 9am-11.30pm Sat, 9am-10.30pm Sun ⊖ Angel
♿ Ⓥ

The House (2, F1)　££
Pub Grub
This renovated pub combines a funky bar with an informal dining room. The menu is strong on seafood dishes such as risotto of calamari with mascarpone, and salt cod *marinière*; it also features excellent salad starters.
☎ 7704 7410 ✉ 63-69

Canonbury Rd N1 ☽ 6-10.30pm Mon, noon-3.30pm & 6-10.30pm Tue-Sat, 6-9.30pm Sun ⊖ Highbury & Islington or ⓡ Essex Rd

Metrogusto (2, F2)　££
Italian
Metrogusto's progressive, modern Italian cuisine – lovingly prepared – draws a good mix of happy diners.
☎ 7226 9400 ✉ 11-13 Theberton St N1 ☽ 6.30-10.30pm Mon-Thu, noon-3pm & 6.30-11pm Fri-Sat, 12.30-3pm Sun ⊖ Angel
♿ Ⓥ

KENSINGTON, KNIGHTSBRIDGE & MAYFAIR

Bibendum (2, D5)　££££
Modern British
This Terence Conran venue is one of London's finest-looking restaurants, set as it is in the Art Nouveau Michelin House (1911), with its magnificent stained-glass windows. The popular Bibendum Oyster Bar is on the ground floor; upstairs is lighter and brighter.
☎ 7581 5817 ✉ 81 Fulham Rd SW3 ☽ noon-2.30pm & 7-11.30pm Mon-Fri, 12.30-3pm &

7-11.30pm Sat, 12.30-3pm & 7-10.30pm Sun ⊖ South Kensington ♿

Boxwood Café (3, A5)　££
European
Gordon Ramsay's attempt to kick back with the young folk and make fine dining a bit more 'relaxed', this New York–style café invites you for a glass of wine or a single course. The starters are the best of the superb food.
☎ 7235 1010 ✉ Berkeley Hotel, Wilton Pl SW1

☽ noon-3pm & 6-11pm ⊖ Hyde Park Corner/Knightsbridge

Daquise (2, B1)　£/££
Polish
This attractively dowdy restaurant is friendly and as authentic as you're likely to find in the centre of London. The varied menu includes many vegetarian and meat dishes, but don't go past the *borscht* (beetroot and bean soup).
☎ 7589 6117 ✉ 20

Thurloe St SW7
🕐 11.30am-11pm
⊖ South Kensington 🚶

Fifth Floor (2, D4) £££
International
This restaurant, bar and café at the Harvey Nichols store is the perfect place to drop after you've shopped. There's a good-value two- and three-course set lunch.
☎ 7823 1839 ✉ Harvey Nichols, 109-125 Knights-bridge SW1 🕐 noon-3pm & 6-11pm Mon-Fri, noon-3.30pm & 6-11pm Sat, noon-3.30pm Sun ⊖ Knightsbridge 🚶 Ⓥ

Gordon Ramsay at Claridge's (3, B4) ££££
European
When the most celebrated chef in London meets its grandest hotel, the result is as close to perfection as you're going to get – even when Ramsay leaves the

Get sated at Bibendum

cooking to his more-than-able protégé Mark Sargeant.
☎ 7499 0099 ✉ 53 Brook St W1 🕐 noon-2.45pm & 5.45-11pm ⊖ Bond St

Isola (2, D4) £££/££££
Italian
With a fancy interior of dark wood, chrome and stainless-steel pillars, Isola also wins accolades as one of the city's best Italian restaurants, with fresh, seasonal ingredients impeccably cooked.
☎ 7838 1044 ✉ 145 Knightsbridge SW1 🕐 noon-3pm & 6-11pm Mon-Sat ⊖ Knightsbridge

Nahm (3, B6) ££££
Thai
Aussie chef and world authority on Thai food David Thompson has won a Michelin star here, combin-ing classic dishes with more exotic fare, such as crab and pomelo with roasted coco-nut and caramel dressing.
☎ 7333 1234 ✉ Halkin Hotel, Halkin St SW1 🕐 noon-2.30pm & 7-11pm Mon-Fri, 7-11pm Sat & Sun ⊖ Hyde Park Corner

Nobu (3, B5) ££££
Japanese
This designer restaurant is known for its superlative black cod. Celebs flock to its minimalist surrounds for

this, as well as the sushi and sashimi.
☎ 7447 4747 ✉ Metro-politan Hotel, 19 Old Park La W1 🕐 noon-2.15pm & 6-10.15pm Mon-Fri, dinner only Sat & Sun ⊖ Hyde Park Corner

The Orangery (2, C4) £/££
Café
This graceful park café in Kensington Gardens is a superb place to have an af-fordable set tea; choose from one with cucumber sand-wiches or scones or the more expensive champagne tea.
☎ 7938 1406 ✉ Ken-sington Gardens W8 🕐 1-6pm Mar-Oct, 1-5pm Nov-Feb ⊖ Queensway 🚶 Ⓥ

On the High Teas
Some of the city's best places to indulge in the English afternoon ritual of tea and scones (or pastries, cucumber sandwiches, teacakes etc) include:
- Claridge's   (p98)
- Fortnum & Mason   (p52)
- The Orangery   (above)
- The Ritz   (p98)
- The Savoy   (p99)

SOUTH LONDON

Asmara (2, F6) £
African
Go Eritrean! The spicy meat and vegetable dishes, served up by staff in trad-itional costumes, are eaten

using a piece of *injera* (a spongy, sour flat bread) as a spoon.
☎ 7737 4144 ✉ 386 Coldharbour La SW9 🕐 5pm-late ⊖ Brixton

Brixtonian Havana Club (2, F6) ££
Caribbean
Zesty Caribbean nosh, a fine array of rum punches and a sociable up-for-it vibe

Golden Oldies

Some places never die, they just become slightly unfashionable. And while the following are no longer at the forefront, they're so well known you might be wondering where to find them:

- **Belgo Centraal** (6, E2 ☎ 7813 2233; 50 Earlham St WC2; ££ ✪ Covent Garden) Mock-monastic Belgian chain serving mussels and french fries.
- **Food for Thought** (6, E2 ☎ 7836 0239; 31 Neal St WC2; £ ✪ Covent Garden) Tiny café and takeaway with wholesome veggie cuisine.
- **Pollo** (6, D2 ☎ 7734 5917; 20 Old Compton St; £ ✪ Leicester Sq) Heaving with customers wanting huge helpings of pasta and tangy red wine.
- **Stockpot** (6, C3 ☎ 7839 5142; 40 Panton St; £ ✪ Piccadilly Circus) Lots of budget comfort food.
- **Yo! Sushi** (6, B2 ☎ 7287 0443; 52 Poland St W1; ££ ✪ Oxford Circus) With this chain, London seems to think it invented the sushi conveyor belt.
- **Wagamama** (3, D3 ☎ 7436 7830; www.wagamama.com; 4a Streatham St WC1; £/££ ✪ Tottenham Court Rd) Sterling noodle-bar chain.
- **Wong Kei** (6, C3 ☎ 7437 3071; 41-43 Wardour St W1; £ ✪ Piccadilly Circus) Cheap Chinese with legendarily rude waiters.

Pining for Goddards' pies

makes this restaurant a perennial local favourite. ☎ 7924 9262 ⊠ 11 Beehive Place SW9; ☽ noon-1am Mon-Thu, noon-2am Fri & Sat, noon-midnight Sun ✪ Brixton

Bug Bar & Restaurant (2, F6)   £/££
Organic
Guilt-free dining in this former church crypt includes organic, vegetarian and free-range. Surrounded by candles, gilt mirrors and ecclesiastical accessories, you tuck into the satisfying mock Cantonese duck, nut Wellington and chicken satay. ☎ 7738 3366 ⊠ St Matthew's Church, Brixton Hill SW2 ☽ 5-11pm

Mon-Thu, 5-11.30pm Fri-Sat, 11am-11pm Sun ✪ Brixton ☕ V

Goddards Pie House (5, A2)   £
British
The standard English fare – steak-and-kidney pies, green peas, jellied eels and

even veggie soy pies – chalked up on the menu of London's oldest pie shop is tops for comfort food. ☎ 8293 9313 ⊠ 45 Greenwich Church St SE10 ☽ 10am-6pm Mon-Thu, 10am-8pm Fri & Sat ☒ Cutty Sark ☕ V

Inside (5, A3)   ££
European
Clean, crisp design meets clean, crisp cuisine, where modern dishes such as fresh-tasting pea soup or truffle and mixed mushroom risotto are served on white linen tablecloths between white and aubergine walls. ☎ 8265 5060 ⊠ 19 Greenwich South St SE10 ☽ noon-2.30pm Wed-Fri, 6.30pm-10pm Mon-Sat, 11am-1.30pm Sat, 11am-3pm Sun ☒ DLR Cutty Sark/Greenwich ☕ V

Blowing them away at Baltic

SOUTH OF THE THAMES

Anchor & Hope (3, F5) £££
Pub Grub

This popular, relatively new gastropub comes from the St John stable (see p66). Accordingly, it's a carnivore's delight.

☎ 7928 9898 ⊠ 36 The Cut SE1 🕑 11am-11pm Tue-Sat, 5-11pm Mon ⊖ Southwark/Waterloo

Baltic (3, F5) £££
Eastern European

The achingly chic bar – with its stainless steel, amber-chip chandelier and up-lit rows of vodkas – gives way to a cavernous, high-ceilinged restaurant. Here, staff in prim grey-and-white uniforms serve up blini, caviar, Georgian lamb shashlik, pork and sauerkraut, Polish black pudding and other delicacies.

☎ 7928 1111 ⊠ 74 Blackfriars Rd SE1 🕑 noon-3pm & 6-11pm Mon-Sat, 6-10.30pm Sun ⊖ Southwark

Konditor & Cook (3, F5) £
Café

Some of the most delightfully sinful chocolate cake (£2.85) this side of Vienna and other sorts of Kuchen are served in this casual caff. Those sans sweet tooth will enjoy its sausage and mash, caesar salad and potato cakes.

☎ 7620 2700 ⊠ 66 The Cut SE1 🕑 8.30am-7.30pm Mon-Fri, 10.30am-7.30pm Sat ⊖ Southwark/Waterloo 🕭 Ⓥ

Laughing Gravy (3, F5) ££
International

Paintings, hanging plants, a large sauce-bottle display and other boho features give gastropub Laughing Gravy (which means whisky) a relaxed living-room feel. The menu is similarly eccentric, mixing unusual ingredients in a surprisingly satisfying way.

☎ 7721 7055 ⊠ 154 Blackfriars Rd 🕑 noon-11pm Mon-Fri, 7pm-midnight Sat ⊖ Southwark

Manze's (3, H6) £
British

If you're looking for a genuine pie and eel shop, Manze's traditionally tiled interior makes it one of London's most aesthetically pleasing. It's handy for Bermondsey Market, too.

☎ 7407 2985 ⊠ 87 Tower Bridge Rd SE1 🕑 11am-2pm Mon, 10.30am-2pm Tue-Thu, 10am-2.15pm Fri, 10am-2.45pm Sat ⊖ Borough/Bermondsey

Oxo Tower Restaurant & Brasserie (3, F4) ££££
International

The famous Oxo Tower is about event dining, with the emphasis more on the event than the food. Magnificent views of the Thames and St Paul's Cathedral guarantee a night to remember. However, the French-with-a-spice-of-Orient cuisine can seem overpriced and the place is often full of suits.

☎ 7803 3888 ⊠ 8th floor, Barge House St SE1 🕑 noon-3pm & 6-11pm Mon-Sat, 6.30-11pm Sun ⊖ Southwark

People's Palace (3, E5) £££
International

Despite the proletarian-sounding moniker, this place attracts an older, upmarket crowd with its modern British cuisine. The white 1950s-style dining room (with early Conran dining chairs) has a high

Feast for the Eyes

The pricey Oxo Tower restaurant (pictured, see above) is renowned for having one of London's best views, but the impecunious can enjoy a similar vista by having a drink in the 7th-floor restaurant or the 4th-floor café of Tate Modern (p9). Other great outlooks are to be had from the People's Palace (above) and Le Pont de la Tour (p76). The Blue Print Café at the Design Museum (see p30) even provides binoculars on every table for diners to gaze close up at Tower Bridge.

ceiling and picture windows overlooking the Thames. ☎ 7928 9999 ✉ Level 3, Royal Festival Hall, South Bank SE1 ⏱ noon-3pm & 5.30-11pm ⊖ Waterloo

People's Palace: all class

Le Pont de la Tour (3, J5) £££
French
It's hardly surprising that Bill and Tony (Clinton and Blair) once dined here. Formal without being intimidating, it boasts an excellent selection of seafood and luscious meat dishes such as chateaubriand – all served within sight of Tower Bridge. ☎ 7403 8403 ✉ Butlers Wharf Building, 36d Shad Thames SE1 ⏱ noon-3pm & 6-11pm Sun-Fri, 6-11pm Sat ⊖ Tower Hill

Tas (3, F5) ££
Turkish
With reliably delicious Anatolian cuisine and straightforward modern surrounds, Tas is deservedly a favourite on this stretch. It complements its fish, grilled meats, couscous and herby casseroles with hummus, tabouli and plump, flavoursome olives. ☎ 7928 1444, 7928 2111 ✉ 33 The Cut SE1 ⏱ noon-11.30pm Mon-Sat, to 10.30pm Sun ⊖ Southwark/Waterloo 👶 Ⓥ

WEST LONDON

The Cow (2, B3) ££
Pub Grub
Opinion is divided as to whether Tom (son of Terence) Conran's gastropub is still the best in town or past its use-by date. Try oysters and Guinness or a pint of prawns and mayonnaise and decide for yourself. ☎ 7221 5400 ✉ 89 Westbourne Park Rd W2 ⏱ food served 12.30-3pm & 6.30-10.30pm ⊖ Westbourne Park/Royal Oak

E&O (2, B3) £££
Asian
One of restaurateur Will Ricker's handful of outlets, E&O (Eastern & Oriental) is all wood-lookalike laminate and white tablecloths in appearance and pan-Asian when it comes to food. Dim sum, sushi, sashimi, tempura, crispy duck and black cod rarely disappoint. ☎ 7229 5454 ✉ 14 Blenheim Crescent

W11 ⏱ 12.15-3pm & 6.15-10.30pm Mon-Sat, 12.15-4pm & 6.15-10pm Sun ⊖ Ladbroke Grove

The Gate (2, A5) ££
Vegetarian
This long-standing vegetarian restaurant is still considered the best in town, not least for its inspired starters and desserts. In an atmospheric location next door to a church, it has a friendly, relaxed vibe. ☎ 8748 6932 ✉ 51 Queen Caroline St W6 ⏱ noon-3pm Mon-Fri, 6-10.45pm Mon-Sat ⊖ Hammersmith 👶 Ⓥ

Geales (2, B4) ££
Seafood
This 65-year old outfit is a fish-and-chip shop deluxe. Everything is priced according to weight and season, which pushes up the price, but, gee, it's worth it. ☎ 7727 7528 ✉ 2

Geales: the real deal

Farmer St W8 ⏱ noon-3pm & 6-11pm Mon-Sat, 6-10.30pm Sun ⊖ Notting Hill Gate 👶

Lucky Seven (2, B3) ££
American
Though pricey, Tom Conran's version of an American diner usually has its vinyl booths full of punters enjoying real meat burgers or a breakfast of pancakes and bottomless cups of coffee. Arrive early or prepare to wait. ☎ 7727 6771 ✉ 127 Westbourne Park Rd W2

🕐 7am-11pm Mon-Sat, 9am-11pm Sun ⊖ Westbourne Park

🕐 noon-11pm Tue-Sun, 6-11pm Mon ⊖ Bayswater 👶 Ⓥ

3pm & 7-9.30pm Mon-Sat ⊖ Hammersmith

Mandola (2, B3) £
African
There's no such thing as popping in for falafel and lime juice in this funky, lo-fi Sudanese café, as everything seems to take time. Still, the likes of *fifilia* vegetable curry and *shorba fule*, an unusual meat and peanut soup, are generally worth the wait.
☎ 7229 4734 ✉ 139-141 Westbourne Grove W2

River Café (2, A6) ££££
Italian
The Fulham set and the new Labour elite still favour this restaurant behind the world-famous cookbooks, so book in advance if you want to treat yourself to its precisely cooked seasonal dishes and river views.
☎ 7381 8824
✉ Thames Wharf, Rainville Rd W6 🕐 12.30-

Sausage & Mash Café (2, B3) £
British
One of the first to exploit the trend for reinventing trad-Brit cuisine, the saucily named S&M chain does dozens of different types of sausages (vegetarian too) and versions of creamy mash.
☎ 8968 8898 ✉ 268 Portobello Rd W10
🕐 11am-10pm Tue-Sun ⊖ Ladbroke Grove 👶 Ⓥ

WEST END CAFÉS

Soho offers the nearest thing London has to a continental café culture. So when you need a break from the crowds thrumming along its streets, duck into one of these.

Bar Italia (6, C2) £
Café
This is the 24-hour opener whose red-eyed, late-night sleaziness was immortalised by Pulp's Jarvis Cocker in the late 1990s. Coffee, Portuguese custard tarts and a 1950s-style custard counter are all 'around the corner where other broken people go'.
☎ 7437 4520 ✉ 22 Frith St W1 🕐 24hr
⊖ Tottenham Court Rd

Maison Bertaux (6, D2) £
Café
Tourists and regulars alike cram into the two tiny floors of this 130-year-old lo-fi café, tempted by its chocolate eclairs and elaborate cakes.
☎ 7437 6007 ✉ 28 Greek St W1 🕐 9am-8pm ⊖ Tottenham Court Rd

Patisserie Valerie (6, C2) £
Café
Proof that you can have your cake and eat it: once you've partaken of one of Valerie's exquisitely iced confections, just carry another home in a ribbon-tied box.
☎ 7437 3466 ✉ 44 Old Compton St W1
🕐 7.30am-8.30pm Mon-Fri, 8am-8.30pm Sat, 9am-6.30pm Sun

⊖ Tottenham Court Rd/Piccadilly Circus

Star Café (6, C1) £
Café
With vintage advertising and Continental European décor, this place is best known among local media workers for its breakfast.
☎ 7437 8778 ✉ 22 Great Chapel St W1
🕐 7am-5pm ⊖ Tottenham Court Rd/Oxford Circus

Valerie's patisseries: kiss your resolve goodbye

Entertainment

Right, this is the bit that many people come to London for, and with several lifetimes needed to exhaust its going-out possibilities, this city doesn't disappoint. It has the best pubs outside Ireland, the best classical ballet outside Russia, and the best English-speaking theatre. That Hollywood stars will take a minimum wage to perform on its stages proves this.

Add a vibrant live-music scene, hip clubs, side-splitting comedy and a rich roster of films and you begin to understand Samuel Johnson's hoary old cliché 'tired of London, tired of life'. Tired of life? No, if you're doing it correctly, you'll simply leave London tired (but happy).

Bookings

Our most pressing advice: wherever possible, book. Things sell out here faster than a Shakespearean actor being offered a lucrative role in a naff Hollywood movie. Theatre and concert-hall box offices open Monday to Saturday from 10am to 8pm or 9pm, but often it's quicker to buy tickets through **Ticketmaster** (☎ 7344 4444; www.ticketmaster.co.uk); a booking fee is charged. This agency also handles music gigs, entrance to larger clubs, comedy shows, sporting fixtures and more.

Last-minute bookers do have a few saviours. The **tkts booth** (6, D3 ☉ 10am-7pm Mon-Sat, noon-3pm Sun ⊖ Leicester Sq) in the clock tower on the southern side of Leicester Square sells half-price tickets to West End theatre shows on the day of a performance, for a reasonable commission. Alternatively, you may be able to get returned tickets from a theatre's box office on the day of the performance. Student stand-by tickets are sometimes available an hour before curtain up.

Of course, there are always touts outside sell-out music gigs, offering tickets for a premium. As with the commercial ticket agencies near Leicester Square advertising half-price theatre tickets without mentioning the high commission charges, do beware of these.

> ### Read All about It
> Details were correct at the time of writing, but prices, club nights and a whole lot more in London changes rapidly, so listings magazine *Time Out* (£2.35; out Tuesday/Wednesday) is always handy, as is the *Metro Life* supplement in the *Evening Standard* newspaper on Thursday.
>
> Visit London has a **London Line** (☎ 09068 663344). It's also worth checking the following sites: www.clubinlondon.co.uk, www.latenightlondon.co.uk and www.pubs.com.

Lost the National Film Theatre? Follow this nifty sign (to p93).

Special Events

Countless festivals and events are held in and around London. Check out Visit London's bimonthly *Events in London* or its *Annual Events* pamphlet; you can also find events listed on its website (www.visitlondon.com).

January *London Parade* – on New Year's Day, Westminster's lord mayor leads a parade of 10,000 musicians and street performers from Parliament Square to Berkeley Square

Late January/early February *Chinese New Year* – lion dances in Soho

March *Oxford & Cambridge Boat Race* – the traditional rowing race on the Thames from Putney to Mortlake

Late March/early April *London Marathon* – the world's biggest road race, with 35,000 participants running 26 miles (42km) from Greenwich Park to the Mall via the Isle of Dogs and Victoria Embankment

May *Chelsea Flower Show* – the world's most famous horticultural show, held at Chelsea Royal Hospital

June *Trooping the Colour* – celebrates the Queen's official birthday with parades and pageantry in Horse Guards Parade, Whitehall

Late June/early July *Wimbledon Lawn Tennis Championships* – runs for two weeks (p96) *City of London Festival* – performances of music, dance, street theatre etc in City churches and squares

July *Hampton Court Palace International Flower Show* – flowers galore in one of London's finest gardens
London Pride March & Mardi Gras – gay and lesbian march from Hyde Park and huge festival in Finsbury Park

July–September *The Proms* – classical music festival at the Royal Albert Hall (p91)

August *Notting Hill Carnival* – a vast Caribbean carnival (one of Europe's biggest outdoor festivals) in Notting Hill on the last Sunday and Monday (bank holiday) of the month

September *London Open House* – general admission, on the third weekend of the month, to some 550 buildings and other sites normally closed to the public
Pearly Harvest Festival Service – brings over 100 Pearly Kings and Queens (East Enders wearing an ornate form of Cockney dress) to a service at St Martin-in-the-Fields (p35)

October–November *Dance Umbrella* – British and international contemporary dance performances at venues across London for five weeks

November *Guy Fawkes Day* – 5 November is the anniversary of an attempted Catholic coup in 1605, with bonfires and fireworks in parks around the city
State Opening of Parliament – the Queen visits Parliament by state coach amid gun salutes
London Film Festival – cinemas in and around Leicester Square and the National Film Theatre, South Bank
Lord Mayor's Show – on the second Saturday in November the newly elected lord mayor travels by state coach from Guildhall to the Royal Courts of Justice, amid floats, bands and fireworks
Remembrance Sunday – on the second Sunday the Queen and government members lay wreaths at the Cenotaph to honour the dead of the two world wars

December *Lighting of the Christmas Tree* – Trafalgar Square

PUBS & BARS

Other countries have pubs, but few can compare to those in the UK. Here, they've had centuries to perfect the art of enjoying a pint in an atmosphere of bonhomie. Most importantly, many pubs still sport the décor of days of yore. For more suggestions, check out Lonely Planet's *London* city guide, the *Time Out Pubs & Bars* guide (£6.99) or www.pubs.com.

The Anchor
Bankside (3, G4)
This higgledy-piggledy 18th-century establishment gazes north across the Thames to the City. It's popular in summer, when customers pour from the interior where lexicographer Dr Johnson once 'worked', heading for the riverside terrace.
☎ 7407 1577 ✉ 34 Park St SE1 ⊖ London Bridge 🍴 (restaurant only)

The Black Friar (3, F4)
This sliver of a building has an Art Nouveau façade, but you still don't guess you're entering one of London's best pubs until you see the mosaics, pillars and fireplaces within. It also has good bitters.
☎ 7236 5474 ✉ 174 Queen Victoria St 🕐 11.30am-11pm Mon-Fri ⊖ Blackfriars

Bluu (3, H1)
This cool industrial bar is one of the bedrocks of the Hoxton scene. Relaunched in 2004, its prime position

makes it an excellent starting point for exploring the area.
☎ 7613 2793 ✉ 1 Hoxton Sq N1 🕐 10am-11.30pm Mon-Thu, 10am-midnight Fri & Sat, noon-10.30pm Sun ⊖ Old St

Café Kick (3, F1)
Three 'baby foot' tables provide the focus of this spartan bar. There's a continental atmosphere, as punters shunt their men around and knock back their beers. Sister venue Bar Kick (3, H1 ☎ 7739 8700; 127 Shoreditch High St E1 ⊖ Old St) has full-sized tables.
☎ 7837 8077 ✉ 43 Exmouth Market EC1 ⊖ Farringdon

Cantaloupe (3, J2)
A forerunner of the hip Hoxton scene, the Cantaloupe has settled back into being a pleasant and unintimidating gastropub.
☎ 7613 4411 ✉ 35-43 Charlotte Rd EC2 🕐 11am-midnight

Café Kick: on the ball

Mon-Fri, noon-midnight Sat, noon-11.30pm Sun ⊖ Old St 🍴 (restaurant only)

The Coach & Horses (6, D2)
'Jeffrey Bernard is unwell,' the *Spectator* magazine would apologise whenever its famous columnist had spent too long AWOL with the other literary soaks, wannabe writers and tourists here.
☎ 7437 5920 ✉ 29 Greek St W1 ⊖ Leicester Sq

Crown & Goose (4, C3)
Just far enough away from Camden Market to feel like a local, this pub offers a laid-back atmosphere between its green walls, plus decently priced beer and food.
☎ 7485 8008 ✉ 100 Arlington Rd NW1 ⊖ Camden Town

Time, Please
London's licensing laws are being relaxed, so pubs could soon have later hours. We've assumed traditional times – Monday to Saturday from 11am (or sometimes noon) to 11pm and Sunday from noon to 10.30pm – and only noted them where they diverge from the norm.

Dreambagsjaguarshoes (3, J1)

This former shoe-and-handbag store is a typical example of Shoreditch shabby-chic, with wooden floors, exposed brick walls, rescued leather sofas and lads wearing just-got-out-of-bed hair.

☎ 7739 9550 ✉ 34-36 Kingsland Rd E2 🕒 5pm-midnight Mon-Fri, noon-midnight Sat, noon-11.30pm Sun ⊖ Old St

Embassy (2, G2)

Islington's hippest DJ bar is full of cool muso and meejah (media) types quaffing beer in the comfy armchairs and sofas, while taking in the chilled vibe.

☎ 7359 7882 ✉ 119 Essex Rd N1 🕒 6-11pm Mon-Thu, 6pm-1am Fri-Sat, 3-10.30pm Sun ⊖ Angel or 🚌 38, 56, 73

French House (6, C2)

This haunt of the Free French during WWII is where to head if you're in the mood for red wine, a half-pint of beer or the company of some eccentric, bohemian characters.

☎ 7437 2799 ✉ 49 Dean St ⊖ Leicester Sq

The Flask (2, C1)

High ceilings, Victorian trimmings and real ale characterise this handy, friendly local.

☎ 7435 4580 ✉ 14 Flask Walk NW3 ⊖ Hampstead 🚻 (till 7pm)

Fluid (3, G2)

Clerkenwell's cool kids enjoy the raspberry-flavoured martinis, freestyle sushi and '70s games machines in this low-lit Japanese-themed bar.

☎ 7253 3444 ✉ 40 Charterhouse St EC1 🕒 noon-midnight Tue & Wed, noon-2am Thu & Fri, 7pm-2am Sat, noon-6.30pm Sun ⊖ Farringdon

The George Inn (3, H5)

London's last surviving galleried coaching inn (built in 1676) certainly merits its National Trust listing. Mentioned in Chaucer's *Canterbury Tales* and Dickens' *Little Dorrit*, today it impresses with its low ceilings and dark-wood fittings.

☎ 7407 2056 ✉ Talbot Yard, 77 Borough High St SE1 ⊖ Borough/London Bridge

Lab (6, C2)

Popular yet stylish cocktail bar in the heart of Soho.

☎ 7437 7820 ✉ 12 Old Compton St W1 🕒 4pm-midnight Mon-Sat, noon-10.30pm Sun ⊖ Tottenham Court Rd/Leicester Sq

The Lamb & Flag (6, E3)

Everyone's 'find' in Covent Garden, this loft-like 17th-century place is always jammed. It's reached through a small alley and has bags of history.

☎ 7497 9504 ✉ 33 Rose St WC2 ⊖ Covent Garden/Leicester Sq 🚻

The Legion (3, H1)

Heavenly Records' achingly cool DJ bars have hit Hoxton, with the usual mix of great jukebox, solid bar food and a pub vibe. Other branches are the media-worker fave Social (3, C3 ☎ 7636 4992; 5 Little Portland St ⊖ Oxford Circus) and the 30-something–friendly Social (2, G2 ☎ 7837 7816; 418 Arlington Sq N1 ⊖ Angel) in Islington.

☎ 7729 441 ✉ 348 Old St 🕒 11am-midnight Mon-Sat, noon-10.30pm Sun ⊖ Old St

Fluid – oozing Japanese kitsch and laid-back cool

Join the tribe at the Vibe Bar and you too could look like this

Loungelover (3, J2)

Evincing the same sparkly, 'junk shop rearranged by a gay stylist' look of its sister establishment Les Trois Garçons (see p71) this bar allows you to indulge in (expensive) drinks among chandeliers, antiques and comfy lounge chairs. Perfect for a celebration.
☎ 7012 1234
✉ 1 Whitby St E1

🕑 6pm–midnight Mon-Sat ⊖ Liverpool St

Market Bar (2, B3)

This deconstructed boho bar is handy if you've been shopping at Portobello Market, but it's a destination in its own right on weekend evenings, when there are DJs. Upstairs is a decent Thai restaurant.
☎ 7229 6472 ✉ 230a Portobello Rd W11
🕑 noon–11pm Mon-Thu, to midnight Fri & Sat, to 10.30pm Sun ⊖ Ladbroke Grove

Mayflower (2, J4)

Shiver me timbers! This historic waterfront pub is named after the ship that took the Pilgrims to America in 1620 from Rotherhithe, and has creaky wooden floors and snugs – allegedly using wood from the same vessel.
☎ 7237 4088 ✉ 117 Rotherhithe St SE16 ⊖ Rotherhithe/Canada Water

Medicine Bar (2, F1)

Surrounded by the generic chains that have overrun Upper St, the original Medicine Bar continues to offer a top night out for grown-up clubbers and their younger mates.
☎ 7704 9536 ✉ 181 Upper St N1 🕑 5pm-midnight Mon-Thu, 5pm-2am Fri, 2pm-2am Sat, 3-10pm Sun ⊖ Highbury & Islington

'Ale & Hearty

Sure, you can order a wine or a cocktail in a London pub, but it's kind of missing the point. In this hard-drinking nation, no-one will argue with the motto 'We're only here for the beer'. The amber liquid generally comes as a pint (570mL) or as a half-pint (285mL). But if you order something on tap (as opposed to in a bottle) you must choose between lager, ale or stout. Lagers are the highly carbonated beers, of medium hop flavour, that are found the world over and drunk cold. Ales, only very slightly gassy, usually have a strong hop flavour and are drunk at room temperature. Fuller's London Pride and Young's are local brands, but when in doubt just order a 'bitter' (a hop-filled beer that tastes more bitter). Stout means a rich, opaque beer like Guinness or Murphy's.

Princess Louise (3, E3)

This Grade II heritage–listed pub is absolutely stunning architecturally, but often packed to its Victorian rafters.
☎ 7405 8816
✉ 208 High Holborn WC1 ☉ closed Sun
⊖ Holborn ♿

Regale your senses at the Princess Louise

The Salisbury (6, D3)

You'll need to brave the crowds at this recently refurbished 1898 pub, to see its beautifully etched and engraved Victorian windows and ornate Art Nouveau light fittings.
☎ 7836 5863 ✉ 90 St Martin's La WC2
⊖ Leicester Sq

Trafalgar Tavern (5, B2)

Once patronised by Charles Dickens and PMs Gladstone and Disraeli (who loved its whitebait), this handsome, but touristy, pub's selling point today is its views of the Thames and the Millennium Dome.
☎ 8858 2437 ✉ Park Row SE10 🚈 DLR Cutty Sark ♿

Vibe Bar (3, J2)

Part bar, part club, the Vibe lets drinkers enjoy themselves in the scuffed leather sofas on quieter nights, but also lets rip frequently with DJs and bands.
☎ 7377 2899 ✉ The Truman Brewery, 91-95 Brick La E1 ☉ 11am-11.30pm Mon-Thu, to 1am Fri & Sat, 11am-10.30pm Sun ⊖ Liverpool St/ Aldgate East

Ye Olde Mitre (3, F3)

Founded in 1546, this is one of London's oldest and most atmospheric pubs – even if it is a bit cramped.
☎ 7405 4751 ✉ 1 Ely Ct, off Hatton Garden EC1 ☉ 11am-11pm Mon-Fri ⊖ Chancery La

CLUBS

Despite the continued success of heavyweight (but clean) club Fabric and scuzzy 333, the general trend has been towards smaller, more salubrious clubs, with several rooms offering different musical styles.

93 Feet East (2, H3)

Why the door heavies? Well, when you've got top Asian underground and electronic nights – plus a great warehouse venue – you wouldn't want to let in anyone uncool. Would you?
☎ 7247 3293 ✉ 150 Brick La E2 £ club £5-10 ☉ club 8pm-2am Thu-Sat, bar 11am-11pm ⊖ Liverpool St

333 (3, J1)

This student-squat style Hoxton club is spread over – surprise! – three floors. Everything from breakbeats and techno to funk happens on the heaving lower two levels. Upstairs is the more chilled Mother bar.
☎ 7739 5949 ✉ 333 Old St EC1 £ club £5-10 ☉ 10pm-5am Fri & Sat, 10pm-4am Sun; Mother Bar 8pm-2am ⊖ Old St

Aquarium (3, H1)

The novelty of a gym-turned-club, complete with pool, was wearing thin until trashy '70s disco Carwash moved in on Saturdays. Dress outrageously retro, but not so outrageously as to include a disco wig, which is specifically banned. Sunday has old-school house, garage and R & B.
☎ 7251 6136, 0870 246 1966 ✉ 256-260 Old St EC1 £ £12-15 ☉ 10pm-3am Sat, 10pm-4am Sun ⊖ Old St

Cargo (3, J1)

The most innovative musical programming in London and a convivial feel under its three brick railway arches propels this bar/restaurant/club into the premier league.
☎ 7739 3440 ✉ 83 Rivington St EC2 £ £5-10 ☉ noon-1am Mon-Thu, to 3am Fri, 6pm-3am Sat, noon-midnight Sun ⊖ Old St

The Cross (2, E2)

In the King's Cross wasteland lies this leading venue, with three floors, a friendly crowd, an outdoor chill-out arena and name DJs, including regular Seb Fontaine.

☎ 7837 0828 ✉ Goods Way Depot, York Way N1 £ £10-15 ⏱ 10.30pm-5am Fri & Sat, 10.30pm-4am Sun ⊖ King's Cross St Pancras

So this is what they mean by *clubbing*...

Egg (2, F1)

Often compared to a club in New York's meat-packing district, on Fridays this designer club has a distinctly polysexual feel.

☎ 7428 7574 ✉ 5-13 Vale Royal, off York Way N1 £ £10-15 ⏱ 10pm-4am Fri, to 5am Sat ⊖ King's Cross St Pancras

The End (6, E1)

This leading West End club has minimalist décor and a hip designer crowd.

☎ 7419 9199 ✉ 18 West Central St WC1 £ £5-15 ⏱ 10pm-3am Mon-Wed, 10pm-4am Thu, 10pm-7am Fri & Sat ⊖ Holborn

Fabric (3, F2)

Super-club lives up to name alert! Punters queue around the corner to gain entry to this smoky warren of three floors, three bars and many walkways – and, of course, to hear the big-name DJs.

☎ 7336 8898, 7490 0444 ✉ 77a Charterhouse St EC1 £ £10-15 ⏱ 9.30pm-5am Fri & Sun, 10pm-7am Sat ⊖ Farringdon

The Fridge (2, F6)

After a decade as one of London's leading venues, the Fridge has been refurbished and reoriented towards a more friendly style of clubbing, with its signature Blast and other evenings.

☎ 7274 2879 ✉ 1 Town Hall Pde, Brixton Hill SW2 £ £10-15 ⏱ 10pm-6am Fri & Sat ⊖ Brixton

Mass (2, F6)

Set in a disused church, complete with vaulted ceilings, pews and frescoes, Mass concentrates on Fetish on Fridays. Saturday is for Dekefex, a mix of drum 'n' bass and hip-hop. The Bug Bar is also here.

☎ 7737 1016 ✉ St Matthew's Church, Brixton Hill SW2 £ club £12-20 ⏱ 10pm-6am Fri & Sat, plus Bug Bar 10pm-2am Thu ⊖ Brixton

Ministry of Sound (3, G6)

No longer just a club but a global brand, the Ministry had a huge revamp in late 2003 to put back a little oomph.

☎ 7378 6528 ⌨ www .ministryofsound.co.uk ✉ 103 Gaunt St SE1 £ £12-15 ⏱ 10.30pm-6am Fri, noon-9am Sat ⊖ Elephant & Castle

---

Three Good Little 'Uns

If super-clubs aren't your style, try one of these:

- **Bar Rumba** (6, C3 ☎ 7287 2715; 36 Shaftes-bury Ave W1 ⊖ Piccadilly Circus) Eclectic music, especially on Mondays, when Gilles Peterson DJs.
- **Cherry Jam** (2, C3 ☎ 7727 9950; 58 Porchester Rd W2 ⊖ Royal Oak) Club nights, including Thursday's Yo-Yo, bands, readings and other arty events.
- **Herbal** (3, J1 ☎ 7613 4462; 10-14 Kingsland Rd E2 ⊖ Old St) Look for the plastic grass on the wall to locate this small, sweaty favourite in the scruffy part of Hoxton.

Notting Hill Arts Club (2, B4)
Ben (Everything But The Girl) Watts' cosy, groovy club garnered attention for Wednesday night's Death Disco, hosted by Creation Records boss Alan McGee and guests, but any night is good.
☎ 7460 4459 ✉ 21 Notting Hill Gate W11
£ £5-6 🕑 6pm-1am Tue-Thu, 6pm-2am Fri & Sat, 4pm-11pm Sun
⊖ Notting Hill Gate

Pacha (3, B6)
This sumptuous outpost of the seminal 'Ibeefa' club – featuring oak panelling, upholstered booths and stained glass – attracts glam customers with soul, funky disco, boogie and hip-hop.
☎ 7834 4440
✉ Terminus Place SW1
£ £20 🕑 10pm-6am Fri & Sat ⊖ Victoria

Studio 33 (2, F5)
One of several new clubs in Vauxhall, this tasteful smaller

Back to School

Funny things, uniform fetishes. And having fuelled a million schoolboy fantasies, they've now inspired a London club night. Every weekend, thousands of punters don a white shirt and tie and hurry to School Disco.

Kissing in the 'snoggers lounge' and other old-skool shenanigans currently alternate between **Sound** (6, C3 ☎ 7287 1010; 10 Wardour St W1 ⊖ Leicester Sq/Piccadilly Circus) on Fridays and **Po Na Na Hammersmith** (2, A5 ☎ 8600 2300; 242 Shepherd's Bush Rd W6 ⊖ Hammersmith) on Saturdays, but it moves around, so double-check listings. Admission costs £10 to £15 and a uniform is compulsory.

---

venue is the new home for the Peach evening of house anthems/trance, which pulls in a young, hedonistic crowd. The Milk after-show party follows in the mornings.
☎ 7820 1702 ✉ 101 Tinworth St, off Albert Embankment SE11
£ £8-12 🕑 10pm-6am Fri, 7am-1pm & 10pm-5am Sat, 7am-1pm Sun
⊖ Vauxhall

Turnmills (3, F2)
This institution on the often chemically fuelled house music scene has added a restaurant on the upper floor.
☎ 7250 3409 ✉ 63 Clerkenwell Rd EC1
£ £8-15 🕑 6pm-midnight Tue, 10.30pm-7.30am Fri, 9pm-1pm Sat, 10pm-6am Sun
⊖ Farringdon

OPEN ALL HOURS

In London, 'open all hours' has always been a relative term, with only clubs and a few other venues staying open much later than 11pm. But the licensing laws have finally been amended and this is changing. Unlike clubs or DJ bars, the venues below don't charge admission. Sometimes, though, food must be ordered if you want to have a drink. (See p64 for a guide to the pricing symbols.)

Cafés & Restaurants

1997 Special Zone (6, C3) £
Hip young post-clubbers head here when they get cravings for Peking duck and comforting soup noodles amid a buzzy vibe.
☎ 7734 2868 ✉ 19

Wardour St W1 🕑 8am-4am ⊖ Piccadilly Circus/Leicester Sq

Café Boheme (6, C2) ££
French-style brasserie where good-looking staff serve meals until the wee hours.
☎ 7734 0623 ✉ 13 Old

Compton St W1 🕑 8am-2.30am Mon-Sat, 8am-11pm Sun ⊖ Tottenham Court Rd/Leicester Sq

Mezzo (6, C2) £££
Ground-floor Mezzonine, serving Asian fusion food, stays open later and is cheaper than the massive

Mezzo, located in the basement and reached via a large spiral staircase.
☎ 7314 4000 🖳 www .conran.com ✉ 100 Wardour St W1 ☽ Mezzo 6pm-12.30am Mon-Thu, to 2.30am Fri & Sat, to 10.30pm Sun; Mezzonine 5.30pm-1am Mon-Thu, to 3am Fri & Sat ⊖ Piccadilly Circus

Pubs & Bars

Bar Soho (6, C2)
Gay and straight pile into this friendly late-opener on one of Soho's main drags.
☎ 7439 0439 ✉ 23-25 Old Compton St W1 ☽ 4pm-1am Mon-Thu, 4pm-3am Fri & Sat, 4pm-12.30am Sun ⊖ Piccadilly Circus/Leicester Sq

Charlie Wright's International Bar (3, H1)
Good beer and a very eclectic mix of late-night characters make this a perfect spot for Hoxton night owls.
☎ 7490 8345 ✉ 45 Pitfield St N1 ☽ noon-1am Mon-Wed, noon-2am Thu-Sun ⊖ Old St 🖘 to 7pm

Service Round the Clock
The following really do open 24/7:

- **Bar Italia** (6, C2) This legendary Italian café (see p77) has a 1950s milk-bar feel.
- **Brick Lane Beigel Bake** (3, J2 ☎ 7729 0616; 159 Brick La E2; ££ ⊖ Old St) Bagels for taxi drivers, clubbers and insomniacs.
- **Old Compton Café** (6, C2 ☎ 7439 3309; 34 Old Compton St W1; £ ⊖ Piccadilly Circus/ Tottenham Court Rd) Myriad sandwiches.
- **Tinseltown** (3, F2 ☎ 7689 2424; 44-46 St John's St EC1; £ ⊖ Farringdon) American-style diner for late-night clubbers and early workers at Smithfield Market.
- **Vingt-Quatre** (2, C5 ☎ 7376 7224; 325 Fulham Rd SW10; ££ ⊖ South Kensington, then bus 14 or 211) Full-service lunches and dinners, but basic fare only after the bar shuts at midnight.

Mash (3, C3)
Über-cool Londoners rate this microbrewery/bar/ restaurant a tad passé, but we still love the downstairs bar and its Marc Newson mural of the bikinied babes who turn out to be girning, not grinning.
☎ 7637 5555 ✉ 19-21 Great Portland St W1 ☽ 11am-midnight Mon & Tue, 11am-2am Wed-Sat ⊖ Oxford Circus

La dolce vita at Bar Italia

ROCK & POP

Whether you want to catch a megastar at Wembley, Earl's Court or the London Arena, the Next Big Thing at a sticky-soled dive or anyone in between, London has arguably the world's best live music scene.

Times given are when you can expect to hear music; venues might be open longer as a pub, club etc.

Mega-Venues

Brixton Academy (2, F6)
A scuzzy but much-loved former theatre, the Academy hosts alternative international and local acts of the ilk of Jet and Massive Attack. Best feature: the sloping (beer-stained) floor, so you can see from the back of a 4000-strong crowd.
☎ 7771 2000 🖳 www .brixton-academy.co.uk ✉ 211 Stockwell Rd SW9 £ £10-20 ☽ varies ⊖ Brixton

Earl's Court Exhibition Centre (2, B5)
The most central London concert arena is slick and

soulless. The acoustics aren't great, but then it's the artists you come to see. ☎ 7385 1200, 0870 903 9033 ⌨ www.eco .co.uk ✉ Warwick Rd SW5 £ £5-50 ☼ varies ⊖ Earl's Court

Mid-Sized

The Forum (2, E1)
This former Art Deco cinema (with a bingo hall–style façade) makes an excellent venue for breakthrough acts. At the time of writing it was also hosting The Church, an infamous antipodean Sunday afternoon of debauchery. ☎ 7344 0044 ⌨ www .meanfiddler. com ✉ 9-17 Highgate Rd NW5 £ £5-15 ☼ varies ⊖ Kentish Town

Hackney Ocean (2, J1)
Despite the vague air of a leisure centre, this venue attracts punters with its salubrious surrounds and fine acoustics. ☎ 8533 0111 ⌨ www .ocean.org.uk ✉ 270 Mare St E8 £ £1-30 ☼ varies ⌨ Hackney Central

Shepherd's Bush Empire (2, A4)
Cleaner than the Forum, this pleasant venue has one weakness – a flat floor that makes it hard to see from the back of the stalls. ☎ 7771 2000 ⌨ www .shepherds-bush-empire .co.uk ✉ Shepherd's Bush Green W12 £ £5-20 ☼ varies ⊖ Shepherd's Bush/Goldhawk Rd

Union Chapel (2, F1)
This octagonal-shaped

Going over the top at Underworld

room is London's most atmospheric venue. The pews and hand-carved banisters are here because it doubles as a church. ☎ 0870 120 1349 ⌨ www.unionchapel .org.uk ✉ Compton Terrace N1 £ £5-20 ☼ varies ⊖ Highbury & Islington

Small but Loud

Barfly@The Monarch (4, B2)
Alternative music radio station Xfm and music weekly *NME* host regular nights at this grungy venue. ☎ 7691 4244, 7691 4245 ⌨ www.barflyclub.com ✉ Monarch pub, 49 Chalk Farm Rd NW1 £ £4-6 ☼ from 7.30pm Tue-Sun ⊖ Chalk Farm

Borderline (6, C1)
This small, relaxed basement bar has a reputation for quality new bands. ☎ 7734 2095 ⌨ www .borderline.co.uk ✉ Orange Yard, off

Manette St W1 £ £5-10 ☼ 8-11pm Mon-Fri ⊖ Tottenham Court Rd

Bull and Gate (2, E1)
A seminal grunge venue. ☎ 7485 5358 ⌨ www .bullandgate.co.uk ✉ 389 Kentish Town Rd NW5 £ £3-5 ☼ 8.30pm ⊖ Kentish Town

Garage (2, F1)
Leading indie guitar-band venue for indie rock from both sides of the Atlantic. ☎ 7607 1818 ⌨ www .meanfiddler.com ✉ 20-22 Highbury Cnr N5 £ £4-10 ☼ 8pm-midnight Mon-Thu, 8pm-3am Fri & Sat ⊖ Highbury & Islington

Underworld (4, C3)
New bands and club nights beneath the huge World's End pub. ☎ 7482 1932 ✉ 174 Camden High St NW1 £ £3-12 ☼ 7pm-3am (nights vary) ⊖ Camden Town

JAZZ

London has always had a thriving jazz scene and, with a recent resurgence led by acid-jazz, hip-hop, funk and swing, it's stronger than ever.

100 Club (6, B1)
Once showcasing the Stones and at the centre of the punk revolution, this legendary London club now concentrates on jazz.
☎ 7636 0933 🖥 www .the100club.co.uk ✉ 100 Oxford St W1 💷 £7-15 🕙 7.45pm-midnight Mon-Thu, noon-3pm & 8.30pm-2am Fri, 7.30pm-1am Sat, 7.30-11.30pm Sun ⊖ Oxford Circus/ Tottenham Court Rd

Jazz Café (4, C3)
It's best to book at this trendy restaurant venue.
☎ 7916 6060 🖥 www .jazzcafe.co.uk ✉ 5-7 Parkway NW1 💷 £10-25 🕙 7pm-1am Mon-Thu, to 2am Fri & Sat, to midnight Sun ⊖ Camden Town

Pizza Express Jazz Club (6, C1)
This small basement venue

Former saxophonist Ronnie Scott lives on

beneath the main chain restaurant goes for big names and the mainstream.
☎ 7439 8722 🖥 www .pizzaexpress.co.uk ✉ 10 Dean St W1 💷 £15-20 🕙 9pm-11.30pm Mon-Thu & Sun, 9pm-midnight Fri & Sat ⊖ Tottenham Court Rd

Ronnie Scott's (6, C2)
Nearly half a century old and having outlived its founder,

this venue is probably the world's most famous jazz club, and has played host to such greats as Miles Davis and Ella Fitzgerald.
☎ 7439 0747 🖥 www .ronniescotts.co.uk ✉ 47 Frith St W1 💷 £20 (members/students Mon-Wed £10/5, Thu-Sun £15) 🕙 8.30pm-3am Mon-Sat, 7.30-10.30pm Sun ⊖ Leicester Sq/Piccadilly Circus

Going It Alone

It can be intimidating travelling solo to a big city, but honestly no-one will look twice if you go out in London alone. In fact, that can be the problem. In a metropolis where 'don't talk to strangers' seems to be a safety message heeded by the entire population, not just children, you'll be lucky if anyone at a concert or bar chats to you. (It does happen, just not as often as elsewhere.)

This anonymity makes solo travellers safe just about anywhere. However, if you don't want to feel conspicuous, eat in a pub or noodle bar, such as **Wagamama** (3, D3 ☎ 7436 7830; www.wagamama.com; 4a Streatham St WC1 ⊖ Tottenham Court Rd), which has branches all over town.

Locals are most likely to talk to you in the pub when there's some sport on the telly, and expat Aussie and South African bars are always convivial. Try **Walkabout** (6, E3 ☎ 7379 5555; 11 Henrietta St WC2 ⊖ Covent Garden) or **Springbok** (6, E3 ☎ 7379 1734; 20 Bedford St WC2 ⊖ Covent Garden). At the theatre and cinema, it's likely you won't be the only one in the audience arriving alone.

FOLK, TRADITIONAL & WORLD MUSIC

Africa Centre (6, E3)
Hosting African music concerts most Fridays, this place hosts other one-offs on Saturdays and weekdays.
☎ 7836 1973 🖳 www.africacentre.org.uk
✉ 38 King St WC2

£ £6-8 ⏲ 11.30pm-3am Fri ➌ Covent Garden/Leicester Sq
♿ varies

Cecil Sharp House (4, B3)
The HQ of the English Folk Dance & Song Society is a good place to acquire a taste for morris dancing and English folk music.
☎ 7485 2206 ✉ 2 Regent's Park Rd NW1
£ £3-6 ⏲ from 7pm (nights vary) ➌ Camden Town ♿ varies

THEATRE

Some 50 theatres in London's West End stage plays such as Agatha Christie's long-running *The Mousetrap*, musicals and hot new hits, and are home to troupes such as the humorous Reduced Shakespeare Company. On top of this are the less commercial, off–West End and fringe theatres, of which a small number are listed here.

Almeida (2, F2)
One of London's best small independent theatre companies, Almeida has attracted the likes of actor Kevin Spacey and director Neil LaBute (*In the Company of Men, Nurse Betty*).
☎ 7359 4404 🖳 www.almeida.co.uk
✉ Almeida St N1
£ £14-25 (stand-by £12) ⏲ varies ➌ Angel/Highbury & Islington

Donmar Warehouse (6, E2)
Where director Sam (*American Beauty*) Mendes persuaded Nicole (theatrical Viagra) Kidman to strip nightly in *The Blue Room*, this tiny theatre still produces challenging drama, with a focus on Continental European plays.
☎ 7369 1732 🖳 www.donmar-warehouse.com
✉ Earlham St WC2
£ £14-242 (stand-by £12) ⏲ varies
➌ Covent Garden

Royal Court (2, D5)
Recent renovations haven't mellowed the Royal Court.

Dramatic Times

Theatre in London has reached a creative peak and it's one of the most compelling reasons to visit the capital right now. Hollywood stars such as Nicole Kidman, Gwyneth Paltrow, Kevin Spacey and Glenn Close have all voted with their manicured feet in recent years, crossing the pond to work for £250 a week. But inspiring artistic directors, extra funds, a wealth of local talent and the West End's decision to adopt some of the experimental attitude of the fringe have played a role, too. That one of London's biggest hits of recent years, *Jerry Springer – The Opera*, started in a small community theatre says it all.

The only tragedy seems to have befallen the esteemed Royal Shakespeare Company. Having moved out of the Barbican and lost a permanent London home, it's now found performing at one or other West End theatre. Check the *Evening Standard* or *Time Out* listings for details.

Having launched *Look Back in Anger* in the 1960s, it still concentrates exclusively on new, exciting playwrights. Just before the performance starts, a small number of standing tickets go on sale for 10p.

☎ 7565 5000 🖳 www .royalcourttheatre.com ✉ Sloane Sq SW1 £ £9.50-26, Mon £7.50 🕓 varies ⊖ Sloane Sq

Royal National Theatre (3, E4)
The nation's flagship theatre has been on a high under artistic director Nicholas Hytner, who has mixed classics with shows by new multicultural authors and downright populist fare. That's gone a long way towards filling the three auditoriums: the Olivier, Lyttleton and Cottesloe.

☎ 7452 3000 🖳 www .nationaltheatre.org.uk ✉ South Bank SE1 £ £10-34 🕓 varies ⊖ Waterloo 🚶 varies

Child's Play
If your kids like puppets, take them to the **Little Angel Theatre** (2, F2 ☎ 7226 1787; 14 Dagmar Passage N1 ⊖ Angel) or the **Puppet Barge Theatre** (2, C3 ☎ 7249 6876; opposite 35 Blomfield Rd W9 ⊖ Warwick Avenue), which tours the country but stays moored in Little Venice in autumn and winter. The **BAC** (Battersea Arts Centre; 2, D6 ☎ 7223 2223; www.bac.org.uk; Lavender Hill SW11 ⊖ Clapham Common or 🚉 Clapham Junction or 🚌 77, 77A or 345) is a community theatre staging innovative plays for all ages, but it, too, has puppet theatre.

For general children's productions, try the **Polka Theatre** (1, C2 ☎ 8543 4888; 240 The Broadway SW19 ⊖ Wimbledon) or the **Unicorn Theatre** (2, F1 ☎ 7700 0702; Pleasance Theatre, Carpenter's Mews, North Rd N7 ⊖ Caledonian Rd).

For more entertainment options for kids, see p40.

SIMON BRACKEN

BALLET & DANCE

Royal Ballet (6, E2)
Stars such as Sylvie Guillem, Irek Mukhamedov, Tamara Rojo and Darcey Bussell pirouette in traditional and modern interpretations of the classics.

☎ 7304 4000 🖳 www .royalballet.co.uk ✉ Royal Opera House, Bow St WC2 £ £4-80 🕓 varies ⊖ Covent Garden

Laban (5, A2)
Dance training, student performances, pieces by the resident Transitions troupe and more take place behind the translucent façade of this award-winning new building by Tate Modern's architects, Herzog and de Meuron.

☎ 8691 8600 🖳 www .laban.org ✉ Creekside SE8 £ £1-15 🕓 varies ⊖ Deptford or 🚉 Greenwich

The Place (3, D1)
The birthplace of modern British dance still stages innovative performances, with Asian influences and a touch of dance theatre.

☎ 7387 0031 🖳 www .theplace.org.uk ✉ 17 Duke's Rd WC1 £ £5-15 🕓 varies ⊖ Euston

Sadler's Wells (3, F1)
This distinguished venue (1683) was last refurbished in 1998. In recent years, it's staged such names as Pina Bausch and Matthew Bourne.

☎ 7863 8000 🖳 www .sadlers-wells.com ✉ Rosebery Ave EC1 £ £10-40 🕓 varies ⊖ Angel

CLASSICAL MUSIC & OPERA

London is home to five symphony orchestras, offering a vast choice, from traditional crowd-pleasers to newer music by 'difficult' composers. Tickets to the opera are costly, but the city's two companies do offer some discounts.

Barbican (3, G2)
It's certainly worthwhile trying to find your way through the Barbican's confusing outer walkways to the auditorium that's home to the prestigious London Symphony Orchestra.
☎ 7638 8891 ▢ www .barbican.org.uk ✉ Silk St EC2 £ £6.50-30, stand-by tickets, students & seniors on day of performance only £6.50-9 ☺ varies ⊖ Moorgate/ Barbican

English National Opera (6, D3)
The ENO presents modern, accessible opera in the breathtaking surrounds of the recently refurbished Coliseum. Same-day, restricted-view tickets are the best deal (£3, but this price is expected to rise).
☎ 7632 8300 ▢ www .eno.org ✉ Coliseum, St Martin's La WC1

Royal Albert Hall: London's answer to the Colosseum

£ tickets £3-65 ☺ varies ⊖ Leicester Sq/Charing Cross

Royal Albert Hall (2, C4)
This splendid, recently revamped Victorian hall hosts classical, rock and other performances, but is best known as the venue for the Proms, which takes place from mid-July to mid-September; see below.
☎ 7589 8212 ▢ www .royalalberthall.com ✉ Kensington Gore SW7

£ tickets £5-150, Proms tickets £4-75 ☺ varies ⊖ South Kensington

Royal Opera House (6, E2)
The once starchy Royal Opera house has been trying to attract a younger, wider crowd in recent years. First came a £210 million redevelopment and the opening up of the Floral Hall to the public in the daytime, with daily tours and free lunchtime concerts on Mondays at 1pm. Now, at certain times of the year, the opera is offering 100 premium seats for just £10 on Mondays.
☎ 7304 4000 ▢ www .royalopera.org ✉ Royal Opera House, Bow St WC2 £ £6-150, midweek matinees £6.50-50 ☺ varies ⊖ Covent Garden

South Bank Centre (3, E4)
The ears have it. The post-war Royal Festival

The Proms

Attending the Proms might render you unable to listen to Elgar's *Land of Hope and Glory* in the same way ever again. That's because this enormous classical music festival often ends with some anachronistic, 'Rule Britannia' flag-waving to the tune. Still, there's an electric atmosphere at the Proms festival. During it, some 1000-odd cheap standing tickets (£4) go on sale an hour before curtain up. Choose whether you want to stand in the gallery or the arena, then join the appropriate (and inevitably long) queue.

Hall (3, E5) is home to two philharmonic orchestras and has superb acoustics. The smaller Queen Elizabeth Hall and Purcell Room attract chamber groups and soloists. ☎ 7960 4242 🖥 www .rfh.org.uk ✉ Belvedere Rd SE1 £ tickets £6-60 🕙 varies ⊖ Waterloo

Wigmore Hall (3, B3)
Its traditional atmosphere, brilliant acoustics and exquisite Art Nouveau detailing make this perhaps London's best classical-music venue. Sunday recitals at 11.30am (£10) are especially good and Monday lunchtime concerts

---

Fresh-Air Culture
London doesn't boast the world's best weather, but that doesn't mean you're always limited to indoor pursuits. When the sun shines, take in a Shakespearean play or a musical at the **Open Air Theatre** (3, A1 ☎ 7486 2431; www.open-air -theatre.org.uk; Regent's Park). For nine weeks in summer a large tent is erected for **Opera Holland Park** (2, B4 ☎ 0845 230 9769; www.operaholland park.com; Holland Park, off Kensington High St W8), while another summer highlight is to attend a classical concert in the grounds of **Kenwood House** (p30).

---

are held at 1pm (£8/6). ☎ 7935 2141 🖥 www .wigmore-hall.org.uk

✉ 36 Wigmore St W1 £ £6-35 🕙 varies ⊖ Bond St

COMEDY

Comedy is bigger in London than in just about any other city we've ever visited. As well as dedicated comedy clubs, many other venues – especially pubs – set aside specific nights for stand-up.

Comedy Café habitués: you have been warned

Comedy Café (3, J1)
Not everyone likes the meal-and-show vibe here, but it gets some good comedians and the Wednesday night try-out spots are excruciatingly entertaining. ☎ 7739 5706 🖥 www .comedycafe.co.uk ✉ 66-68 Rivington St

EC2 £ Wed free, Sat up to £14 🕙 Wed-Sat ⊖ Old St

Comedy Store (6, C3)
The spiritual home of English alternative comedy (think Ben Elton and crew) has been in existence since Margaret Thatcher was in power and has long

outstayed the old battle-axe. ☎ 7344 4444 🖥 www .thecomedystore.co.uk ✉ 1a Oxendon St SW1 £ £13/8 🕙 Tue-Sun ⊖ Piccadilly Circus

Jongleurs (4, B2)
This chain churns out the jokes as if they were fast-food burgers to go, but the punters love it, so you should book ahead. The bill normally features one fantastic, big-name comic and a couple of jokesters on unicycles (or similar). Other branches are at Battersea and Bow (see the website for details). ☎ 0870 787 0707 🖥 www.jongleurs.com ✉ 11 East Yard NW1 £ £15 🕙 Fri & Sat ⊖ Camden Town

CINEMAS

Multiplexes have invaded London, but some great independent cinemas remain. Full-price tickets cost £8.50 to £12 for a first-run film; an afternoon weekday session and anytime on Monday is usually cheaper (£4 to £5.50).

Curzon Soho (6, D2)
Simply the best all-round cinema in central London, with great art-house/indie programming and two convivial bars.
☎ 7439 4805 (information), 7734 2255 (bookings) 🖳 www.curzoncinemas.com ✉ 93-107 Shaftesbury Ave W1 ⊖ Leicester Sq/Piccadilly Circus

Electric Cinema (2, B4)
This Edwardian cinema is luxuriously fitted out with leather armchairs (£12.50, or £30 for a two-seater sofa) footstools and tables for food and drink. It's a Rolls Royce of movie-houses.
☎ 7908 9696, 7229 8688 🖳 www.the-electric

.co.uk ✉ 191 Portobello Rd W1 ⊖ Ladbroke Grove/Notting Hill Gate

National Film Theatre (3, E4)
Britain's national repository of film is a magnet for cinephiles, whether it's inviting directors to introduce their new releases or dusting off golden oldies for retrospectives.
☎ 7928 3232 🖳 www.bfi.org.uk/nft ✉ South Bank SE1 ⊖ Waterloo/Embankment

Prince Charles Cinema (6, D3)
Self-confessed movie geeks love the late-night Prince Charles. Where else can you gorge on cult classics for £2.50 to £3.50 or sing

An eye-opening experience

along with the rest of the audience to *The Sound of Music* (7.30pm Friday, admission £13.50)?
☎ 0901 272 7007 (information, 25p per min), 7494 3654 (bookings) ✉ Leicester Place WC2 ⊖ Leicester Sq

GAY & LESBIAN LONDON

Local gays and lesbians might complain that the scene is too commercial or superficial, but intolerant attitudes from other Londoners are rarely a problem.

The Astoria (6, C1)
G-A-Y evenings dominate this dark, sweaty club. Saturday is the flagship night, but there's a cheap Pink Pounder on Monday, pop and house Music Factory on Thursday and disco-orientated Camp Attack on Friday. There's also a G-A-Y Bar (6, C2; 30 Old Compton St 🕓 daily).
☎ 7434 9592, 7434 6963 🖳 www.g-a-y.co.uk ✉ 157 Charing Cross Rd

WC2 🕓 10.30pm-4am Mon & Thu, 11pm-4am Fri, 10.30pm-5am Sat ⊖ Tottenham Court Rd

Crash (2, F5)
This muscle-boy mecca has two floors churning out hard beats, four bars and even a few go-go dancers.
☎ 7820 1500 ✉ 66 Goding St SE11 🕓 10.30pm-6am Sat ⊖ Vauxhall

Wear it loud, wear it proud

DTPM@Fabric (3, F2)
The name, apparently Drugs Taken Per Minute, makes sense when you see the wired, hedonistic crowd. Superb venue, too (see p84). ☎ 7336 8898, 7490 0444 ✉ 77a Charterhouse St EC1 £ £11-15 ☽ 9.30pm-5am Sun ⊖ Farringdon

Fiction@The Cross (2, E2)
Huge queues form for this classic house evening at one of London's best venues (see p84). So arrive early. ☎ 7837 0828 ✉ Goods Way Depot, York Way N1 £ £9-11 ☽ 10.30pm-5am Fri ⊖ King's Cross St Pancras

The Ghetto (6, C1)
London's gay venue du jour hosts not only the celebrity-attended mixed evening Nag, Nag, Nag on Wednesday, but also Friday's electro/pop The

Scene in Soho
Soho, particularly in and around Old Compton St, remains the heart of gay London's café scene.
- **Balans** (6, C2 ☎ 7437 5212; 60 Old Compton St W1 ⊖ Piccadilly Circus/Leicester Sq) A continental-style café, open to the wee hours.
- **Candy Bar** (6, C2 ☎ 7494 4041; 23-24 Bateman St W1 ⊖ Tottenham Court Rd) Fave lesbian bar.
- **First Out** (6, D1 ☎ 7240 8042; 52 St Giles High St WC2 ⊖ Tottenham Court Rd) Laid-back veggie café.
- **Freedom** (6, C2 ☎ 7734 0071; 60-66 Wardour St W1 ⊖ Piccadilly Circus) Increasingly mixed modern café-bar.
- **Rupert St** (6, C2 ☎ 7292 7141; 50 Rupert St W1 ⊖ Piccadilly Circus) Large glass windows make this a place to pose and preen.

Cock, among others. It's popular with Muscle Marys, trannies, punks and polysexual fashionistas. ☎ 7287 3726 ✉ 5-6 Falconberg Ct W1 £ £3-6 ☽ 10pm-3am Mon-Thu, from 10.30pm Wed,

10.30pm-4.30am Fri & Sat ⊖ Tottenham Court Rd

Heaven (6, E4)
One of the world's best-known gay clubs lets you choose between, say, cheap drinks and lack of pretension at Monday's Popcorn and the commercial house music of Saturday's flagship evening. ☎ 7930 2020 ✉ Under the Arches, Villiers St WC2 £ £2-12 ☽ 10.30pm-3am Mon & Wed, 10pm-3am Fri, 10pm-5am Sat ⊖ Embankment/Charing Cross

Popstarz@The Scala (3, E1)
This long-running alternative gay evening has put one of London's old cinemas to good use. Three dance floors play indie, '80s and '90s pop and R & B. ☎ 7833 2022 ✉ 275 Pentonville Rd N1 £ £4-8 ☽ 10pm-5am Fri ⊖ King's Cross St Pancras

Strike a pose at Rupert St

Gay & Lesbian News
In the gay cafés, bars and clubs listed, you should find the relatively political *Pink Paper* (free) and, for listings, *Gay Times* (£3.10), *Boyz* (free) and the lesbian *Diva* (£2.65). The gay sections of *Time Out* and the *Evening Standard's Metro Life* are also useful, as are websites www.rainbownetwork.com for men and www.gingerbeer.co.uk for women.

SPORTS

Athletics

Athletics meetings attracting international and UK stars take place during summer at the **Crystal Palace National Sports Centre** (1, C2 ☎ 8778 0131; www.crystalpalace.co.uk; Ledrington Rd SE19 🚇 Crystal Palace).

Cricket

Despite a so-so England team, cricket remains popular. Test matches take place at **Lord's Cricket Ground** (2, C2 ☎ 7432 1066; www.lords.org; St

Lord's Cricket Ground media centre

John's Wood Rd NW8 ⊖ St John's Wood) and at the **Oval Cricket Ground** (2, F6 ☎ 7582 7764; www .surreyccc.co.uk; Kennington Oval SE11 ⊖ Oval). Lord's test tickets are £25 to £50 and go fast, but extra seats are released three weeks before a match. The Oval booking office opens only during the April to September season. Tests cost £45 or £10 (fifth day). County fixtures cost £5 to £10.

Football

London has a dozen league teams, half of them in the UK Premier League. So any Wednesday or weekend from August to mid-May, quality football is just a tube ride away, if you can get a ticket. The two most publicised teams are the mega-successful Arsenal (set to have a new stadium by 2006) and Chelsea, the latter now bankrolled by expat Russian oligarch Roman Abramovich.

Arsenal's current stadium

Wembley Stadium in northwest London, where the England team has traditionally played international matches and the FA Cup Final has been held in mid-May, is due to reopen in 2006. The final has been held in Cardiff in recent years.

Fever Pitch

Phone for match details or credit-card bookings:

- **Arsenal** (☎ 7704 4000/7413 3366; www.arsenal.com)
- **Charlton Athletic** (☎ 8333 4000/8333 4010; www.charlton-athletic.co.uk)
- **Chelsea** (☎ 7385 5545/7386 7799; www.chelseafc.co.uk)
- **Fulham** (☎ 7893 8383/7384 4710; www.fulhamfc.co.uk)
- **Tottenham Hotspur** (☎ 8365 5000/0870 420 5000; www.spurs.co.uk)
- **West Ham** (☎ 8548 2748/8548 2700; www.westhamunited.co.uk)

Racing

Plenty of top-quality horse racecourses are within striking distance of London, including **Ascot** (☎ 01344-622211; www.ascot.co.uk) in Berkshire and **Epsom** (☎ 01372-470047; www.epsomderby.co.uk) in Surrey. The flat-racing season runs from April to September.

Looking for a cheap (£1.50 to £5 for a 12-race meeting) and thrilling night at the races? Consider going to the dogs. There's greyhound racing at **Walthamstow Stadium** (☎ 8531 4255; www.wsgreyhound.co.uk; Chingford Rd E4 ® Highams Park).

Rugby Union & Rugby League

Rugby union focuses on southwest London, with teams such as the Wasps, Harlequins and London Welsh playing from August to May. Each January to March, there's the Six Nations Championship between England, Scotland, Wales, Ireland, France and Italy. The English game's shrine is **Twickenham Rugby Stadium** (1, B2 ☎ 8892 2000; www.rfu.com; Rugby Rd, Twickenham ⊖ Hounslow East, then bus 281 or rail Twickenham).

The only local rugby league side is the **London Broncos** (5, C1 ☎ 8853 8001; www.londonbroncos.co.uk; the Valley, Floyd Rd SE7 ® Charlton).

Tennis

The All England Lawn Tennis Championships have been held in late June/early July since 1877 at **Wimbledon** (1, C1 ☎ 8944 1066, 8946 2244; www.wimbledon.org; Church Rd SW19 ⊖ Southfields/Wimbledon Park). Most tickets for the Centre and Number One courts are distributed by ballot. Applications must be made between 1 September and 31 December the preceding year; send a stamped self-addressed envelope to All England Lawn Tennis Club, PO Box 98, Church Rd, Wimbledon SW19 5AE. Otherwise, try to book as early as possible. Limited tickets (around £50) are sold the day of play, if you can face the dreadful queues. Prices for outside courts cost less than £10, reduced after 5pm. The warm-up tournament at **Queen's Club** (☎ 7385 3421; www.queensclub.co.uk; Palliser Rd W14 £ per day £12 ⊖ Baron's Court) is easier to get into.

Pretty in pink? Gone to the dogs at Walthamstow

Sleeping

The Ritz, the Dorchester, the Savoy – London has some world-renowned hotels, and yet accommodation remains the thorniest issue in arranging a stay here. Simply, it's so expensive. Some websites, including Visit London's www.visitlondonoffers.com do have good last-minute deals, but the quickest solution to the accommodation conundrum is to take a deep breath, reach deep into your wallet and square it all with the bank manager later.

That aside, it's wise to choose to stay in the area where you'll be spending the most time. Distance and traffic mean it can take ages to cross town, so if you're planning to explore the rejuvenated areas of Hoxton and Clerkenwell, for example, it's hardly worthwhile booking a hotel in Notting Hill.

Bloomsbury is an accommodation hot spot, due to its proximity to the British Museum and Oxford St, and South Kensington also caters amply to tourists. But there are few places in central London where you're far from a hotel.

Value for money is still largely lacking in the mid-range bracket. However, in recent years, designer lodgings such as St Martin's Lane, Sanderson and the Great Eastern have shaken up the top end of the market, while budget brands such as Travel Inn and Express by Holiday Inn are helping the city to lose its rip-off tag. You can also get high-quality accommodation for reasonable prices by staying weekends in the financial district of the City.

With London holding its own in a relatively stay-at-home era, demand for hotel rooms can still outstrip supply, especially in summer (when rates rise by up to 25%) and especially at the bottom end of the market. So it's worth booking at least a night or two before you arrive. Single rooms are in particularly short supply.

Room Rates	
These categories indicate the cost per night of a standard double room in high season.	
Deluxe	from £300
Top End	£150 to £300
Mid-Range	£85 to £150
Budget	under £85

Booking Services

Free same-day accommodation bookings can be made at most tourist information centres (see p122). **Visit London** (☎ 08456 443 010; www.visitlondonoffers.com) has good deals. Also worth a try are:

- **British Hotel Reservation Centre** (☎ 7340 1616; www .bhrconline.com; Victoria Station; £3).
- **First Option** (per booking £5) There are kiosks at the Britain Visitor Centre (p122); Euston (☎ 7388 7435), King's Cross St Pancras (☎ 7837 5681), Victoria (☎ 7828 4646) and Gatwick Airport (☎ 01293-529372) train stations; and South Kensington tube station (☎ 7581 9766).
- B&B booking services, which charge booking fees and include **At Home in London** (☎ 8748 1943; www.athomeinlondon.co.uk), **London Bed & Breakfast Agency** (☎ 7586 2768; www.londonbb.com), **London Home to Home** (☎ 8567 2998; www.londonhometohome.com) and **Uptown Reservations** (☎ 7351 3445; www.uptownres.co.uk). Often a surcharge applies for stays of less than three nights.

DELUXE

Blakes (2, C5)

Although each room is decorated as a separate fantasy, there's a colonial touch throughout London's original boutique hotel. Four-poster beds, lacquered chests, striped cushions, draped fabrics and antiques all keep it a connoisseur's favourite. And who could say 'Not tonight, Josephine' in the bed that once belonged to Napoleon's consort?
☎ 7370 6701 🖳 www .blakeshotel.com ✉ 33 Roland Gardens SW7, South Kensington ⊖ Gloucester Rd ⊠ Blakes

Claridge's (3, B4)

Probably London's greatest five-star hotel, Claridge's is a cherished reminder of a bygone era. Art Deco dominates the public areas and 203 rooms and suites; some of the 1930s furniture once graced the staterooms of the decommissioned SS *Normandie*.
☎ 7629 8860 🖳 www .claridges.co.uk ✉ 53-55 Brook St W1 ⊖ Bond St ⊠ Gordon Ramsay, p73

No 5 Maddox St (6, A2)

This suite hotel is meant to feel like your own rented pad, and we wouldn't mind a home like this, with its natural tones, Eastern themes and suede sofas. Each suite has its own kitchen and free broadband Internet. A great urban sanctuary.
☎ 7647 0200 🖳 www .living-rooms.co.uk ✉ 5 Maddox St W1 ⊖ Oxford Circus

Join the inner circle in the lobby of Threadneedles hotel

JONATHAN SMITH

One Aldwych (6, F3)

With muted earthy tones and exposed bathroom sinks, One Aldwych was one of the first of London's new designer hotels. Its two restaurants and fabulous fitness centre make it a hit with the in crowd.
☎ 7300 1000 🖳 www .onealdwych.co.uk ✉ 1 Aldwych WC2 ⊖ Holborn ⊠ Axis, Indigo

The Ritz (3, C4)

The name has become synonymous with luxury, and the grandiloquent Palm Court tearoom puts on the ritz indeed. Rococo-style rooms feature silk bedspreads, brocade drapes, gold-leaf trimmings and marble bathrooms.
☎ 7493 8181 🖳 www .theritzlondon.com ✉ 150 Piccadilly W1 ⊖ Green Park ⊠ Ritz restaurant, Palm Court (afternoon tea)

St Martin's Lane (6, D3)

By day, the glass façade

Extra Opulence

Here are some other 'names' among London's vast array of luxury hotels:

- **Dorchester** (3, A4 ☎ 7629 8888; www.dorches terhotel.com; Park La W1 ⊖ Hyde Park Corner) Offering Georgian country-house rooms, views of Hyde Park and the most opulent lobby in town.
- **Lanesborough** (3, A5 ☎ 7259 5599; www.lanes borough.com; Hyde Park Corner SW1 ⊖ Hyde Park Corner) A business favourite for its mix of opulent Regency furnishings and state-of-the-art technology, including in-room computers.
- **Metropolitan** (3, B5 ☎ 7447 1000; www.met ropolitan.co.uk; Old Park La SW1 ⊖ Green Park/ Hyde Park Corner) The epitome of contemporary minimalism, known for its exclusive Met Bar and Nobu restaurant (see p73).

of this achingly hip Ian Schrager-Philippe Starck creation is blank and discreet. By night, as guests use the switch by their bed to cast a coloured glow over their white room, it can resemble a disco-style checkerboard. Popular with models and fashionistas.
☎ 7300 5500 🖳 www .ianschragerhotels.com ✉ 45 St Martin's La WC2 ⊖ Leicester Sq/Charing Cross ✖ Asia de Cuba

The Savoy (6, F3)
Between the landmark Strand-side entrance – the only London street where traffic drives on the right – and the Art Deco façade facing the River Thames lie rooms so luxurious and with such great views that some guests have taken up permanent residence.
☎ 7836 4343 🖳 www .savoy-group.co.uk ✉ Strand WC2 ⊖ Charing Cross ✖ The Savoy

Grill, the Thames Foyer (afternoon tea)

Threadneedles (3, H3)
Through the amazing circular lobby – with its 19th-century painted glass dome – lie elegant, contemporary rooms with a distinctly masculine tone. The City location means good weekend rates.
☎ 7657 8080 🖳 www .theetoncollection.com ✉ 5 Threadneedle St EC2 ⊖ Bank ✖ Bonds

TOP END

Charlotte Street (3, C3)
Laura Ashley goes post-modern and comes up smelling of roses in this favourite of visiting media types.
☎ 7806 2000 🖳 www .charlottestreethotel.com ✉ 15-17 Charlotte St W1 ⊖ Goodge St ✖ Oscar

Gore (2, C5)
The 54 opulent rooms of these Victorian townhouses are kitted out with polished mahogany, Turkish carpets, antique-style bathrooms, potted aspidistras and 5000 portraits and prints.
☎ 7584 6601 🖳 www .gorehotel.co.uk ✉ 189 Queen's Gate SW7 ⊖ High St Kensington/Gloucester Rd ✖ Bistrot 190

Great Eastern Hotel (3, J3)
This 267-room hotel is just the right mix of hip and classic. Accommodation on the lower floors has a more masculine feel, with dark wood and red, earthy tones; rooms on the upper floors flirt with a subtle maritime theme. Arne Jacobsen

lamps and Eames chairs help make it a style winner.
☎ 7618 5000 🖳 www .great-eastern-hotel.co.uk ✉ Liverpool St EC2 ⊖ Liverpool St ✖ Aurora, Miyabi and Fishmarket restaurants, Terminus brasserie

Hazlitt's (6, C2)
A private hideaway in the heart of Soho, these three Georgian houses have 23 rooms decorated with antique furniture and prints.
☎ 7434 1771 🖳 www .hazlittshotel.com ✉ 6 Frith St, Soho Sq W1 ⊖ Tottenham Court Rd ✖ Central London (p67)

Malmaison (3, G2)
The modern Scottish

JONATHAN SMITH

The hip Great Eastern Hotel

boutique chain has brought that rare London thing (value for money) to Clerkenwell. Weekend prices (from £99) are in the moderate range.
☎ 7012 3700 🖳 www .malmaison.com ✉ Charterhouse Sq EC1 ⊖ Farringdon/Barbican ✖ The Brasserie

---

Accommodation Guides
Visit London's *Where to Stay & What to Do in London* (£4.99) lists approved hotels, guesthouses, apartments and B&Bs, and publishes the free *Where to Stay on a Budget*. Useful websites include www.frontdesk.co.uk, www.hotelsoflondon.co.uk, www.London.nethotels .com and www.londonlodging.co.uk .

myhotel bloomsbury (3, C3)

Who would have thought minimalism and Orientalism would make such a good match? But the Asian accessories perfectly complement the dark wood and bright fabrics, while rooms are organised according to the principles of Feng Shui.
☎ 7667 6000 ☐ www .myhotels.co.uk ✉ 11-13 Bayley St WC1 ⊖ Goodge St ✗ Yo Sushi!

Number Sixteen (2, C5)

Still one of the best of hoteliers Kit and Tim Kemp's Firmdale boutique chain (check website for others), this garden townhouse encapsulates Firmdale's warm, modern English style. An honour bar for guests and a relaxed vibe complete the winning package.
☎ 7589 5232 ☐ www .firmdale.com ✉ 16 Sumner Pl SW7 ⊖ South Kensington

✗ Kensington, Knightsbridge & Mayfair (pp72-3)

Portobello (2, B4)

Mythologised as the place where the maid mistook Kate Moss and Johnny Depp's champagne bath for dirty water in number 16, the funky Portobello continues to check in rock stars, film stars and models.
☎ 7727 2777 ☐ www .portobello-hotel.co.uk ✉ 22 Stanley Gardens W11 ⊖ Notting Hill Gate ✗ West London (pp76-7)

Rookery (3, F2)

Floors slope and lean in this once-derelict row of 18th-century Georgian houses, which only adds to the charm. Period furniture includes some claw-foot Victorian baths.
☎ 7336 0931 ☐ www .rookeryhotel.com ✉ Peter's La, Cowcross St EC1 ⊖ Farringdon

✗ Bloomsbury & Clerkenwell (pp65-6)

Sanderson (3, C3)

The interior of this Phillipe Starck—designed hotel is distinguished by its modern furniture – including a Dali-style Mae West lips sofa in its lobby. A mere curtain or sheet of glass separates white bedrooms from their bathrooms.
☎ 7300 1400 ☐ www .ianschragerhotels.com ✉ 50 Berners St W1 ⊖ Oxford Circus ✗ Spoon+

Slickly Starck Sanderson

MID-RANGE

Crescent (3, D1)

Overlooking a private square in north Bloomsbury, this friendly, family-owned hotel ensures all its rooms are spick and span – whether they be tiny singles with shared facilities or spacious doubles with private bathrooms.
☎ 7387 1515 ☐ www .crescenthoteloflondon .com ✉ 49-50 Cartwright Gardens WC1 ⊖ Russell Sq/Euston

Durrants (3, A2)

The same family has owned this gem since 1921 and its uniformed staff and traditional décor mean it exudes olde-worlde English charm. Just creeping into the mid-range bracket, it's handy for a spot of Oxford St shopping.
☎ 7935 8131 ☐ www .durrantshotel.co.uk ✉ George St W1 ⊖ Bond St/Baker St

Express by Holiday Inn (3, H1)

With its blue-and-yellow linen, blonde wood and glass bricks, this mid-priced chain delivers great value for money and feels more personable than you might expect. Other Holiday Inn Express hotels in London include a Southwark branch behind Tate Modern (3, G5 ☎ 7401 2525; 103-109 Southwark St SE1 ⊖ Southwark).
☎ 7300 4300 ☐ www .hiexpress.co.uk ✉ 275 Old St EC1 ⊖ Old St ✗ &

Fielding (6, E2)

Its rooms are small and its furnishings shop bought, but just a block away from the Royal Opera House you can really feel the pulse of the West End in this small hotel. ☎ 7836 8305 🖳 www .the-fielding-hotel.co.uk ✉ 4 Broad Court, off Bow St WC2 ⊖ Covent Garden ⌘ Central London (p67)

Guesthouse West (2, B3)
With grey blankets folded across the bottom of white duvets, orchids and muted toffee-coloured bathrooms, this new-ish establishment provides a fashionable take on the B&B concept. The vintage 1950s film posters in the bar are another distinctive touch.
☎ 7792 9800 🖳 www .guesthousewest.com ✉ 163-165 Westbourne Grove W11 ⊖ Westbourne Park/Royal Oak ⌘ West London (pp76-7)

Morgan Hotel (3, D3)
Its handy location near the British Museum and its efficient double-glazing help make this well-furnished hotel one of London's best mid-priced options. The warmth and hospitality more than compensate for the modest size of the rooms.
☎ 7636 3735; fax 7636 3735 ✉ 24 & 40 Bloomsbury St WC1 ⊖ Tottenham Court Rd ⌘ Central London (p67)

Pavilion (2, C3)
Every city needs a glam, reasonably priced hotel like this. The Moorish Casablanca Nights is the most popular of the 30 opulent and individually themed rooms, which also include Enter the Dragon (chinoiserie) and Highland Fling (Scottish).
☎ 7262 0905 🖳 www .pavilionhoteluk.com ✉ 34-36 Sussex Gardens W2 ⊖ Edgware Rd/ Paddington

St Margaret's (3, D2)
This 60-room, family-run hotel is set in a classic Georgian terrace and caters for all ages. There are relaxing lounges and a lovely rear garden.
☎ 7636 4277 🖳 www .stmargaretshotel.co.uk ✉ 26 Bedford Place WC1 ⊖ Russell Sq

Swiss House (2, C5)
Wooden furniture, white walls and navy linen in the 17 rooms create the sort of unpretentious alpine freshness that one would expect from something called *Swiss*. It's handy for South Kensington, too.
☎ 7373 2769 🖳 www .swiss-hh.demon.co.uk ✉ 171 Old Brompton Rd SW5 ⊖ Gloucester Rd

Opulence à la Pavilion

Vicarage (2, B4)
Gilt mirrors, chandeliers and gold-and-red-striped wallpaper wow guests as they enter this former Victorian private house. The rooms are a little less lavish, but just as atmospheric. Rooms on the higher floors have shared bathrooms and budget prices. If it's full, try the humble but pleasant Abbey House (☎ 7727 2594; www.abbeyhousekensing ton.com) next door.
☎ 7729 4030 🖳 www. londonvicaragehotel.com ✉ 10 Vicarage Gate W8 ⊖ High St Kensington/ Notting Hill Gate ⌘ West London (pp76-7) ♿

Windermere (2, E5)
Named by Visit London in 2003 as the capital's best B&B, the family-run, warren-like Windermere is cosy and full of character. Eight of the 22 small, individually designed rooms are nonsmoking.
☎ 7834 5163 🖳 www.windermere -hotel.co.uk ✉ 142- 144 Warwick Way SW1 ⊖ Victoria ⌘ Pimlico Room ♿

Serviced Apartments
If you prefer to rent a flat rather than stay in a hotel, agencies worth contacting include: **Aston's Budget & Designer Studios** (☎ 7590 6000; www.astonsap artments.com) and **London Holiday Accommoda- tion** (☎ 7485 0117; www.londonholiday.co.uk). Costs can range from anywhere between £35 to £90 per night for a double to £600 per week, and £800 to £1100 per week for a quad.

BUDGET

Hampstead Village Guesthouse (2, C1)

In this charming B&B, you stay with an Anglo-Dutch family and their dog. With rustic décor throughout, rooms sometimes have their own freestanding tub or a roof terrace. There's also a family apartment and a lovely back garden.

☎ 7439 8679 ⬛ www .hampsteadguesthouse .com ✉ 2 Kemplay Rd NW3 ⊖ Hampstead ✗ Camden & Hampstead (p66) ♿

Hyde Park Rooms (2, C3)

There's a hippy, homy feel to this immaculately kept abode, with Persian carpets in its tiled entrance hall, vaguely Asian lampshades and the friendly proprietor's own art on the walls.

☎ 7723 0965 ⬛ www .hydeparkroomshotel.com ✉ 137 Sussex Gardens W2 ⊖ Paddington

Garden Court (2, B4)

It's the little things that make this well-run, well-kept family hotel stand out – like the Beefeater statue in the lounge. Each of its 34 rooms has phone and TV, though they just scrape into this price category.

☎ 7229 2553 ⬛ www .gardencourthotel.co.uk ✉ 30-31 Kensington Gardens Sq W2 ⊖ Bayswater ✗ West London (pp76-7) ♿

Luna & Simone Hotel (2, E5)

By taking the décor of a mid-range chain and adding contemporary art and slate-tiled modern bathrooms, this 35-room place has turned itself into a superlative, if compact, budget hotel.

☎ 7834 5897 ⬛ www .lunasimonehotel.com ✉ 47 Belgrave Rd SW1 ⊖ Victoria ♿

Portobello Gold (2, B4)

A restaurant-bar with a few rooms attached, Portobello Gold is certainly special. Three comfy rooms can be cunningly converted into offices by day; of the other three, one is a basic backpackers twin room.

☎ 7460 4913 ⬛ www .portobellogold.com

In the groove at Generator

✉ 95-97 Portobello Rd W11 ⊖ Notting Hill Gate ✗ Portobello Gold restaurant

Stylotel (2, C3)

Among the chintzy hotels on Sussex Gardens, this place presents clean, modern design at budget prices. Rooms have lots of blue, stainless-steel features and capsule bathrooms.

☎ 7723 1026 ⬛ www .stylotel.com ✉ 160-162 Sussex Gardens W2 ⊖ Paddington

Travel Inn County Hall (3, E5)

Purple paint, vinyl flooring, vending machines and laminated menus make this the McDonalds of the hotel world. Still, at £85 for a family room in such an ideal location, who'd complain? Check the website for other London branches, including the Euston Travel Inn Capital (3, D1 ☎ 7554 34001; Dukes Rd WC1 ⊖ Euston).

☎ 7902 1600 ⬛ www .travelinn.co.uk ✉ Belvedere Rd SE1 ⊖ Westminster ✗ Potter's Bar & Restaurant ♿

Hostels

Given London's high costs, travellers on a budget will prefer independent hostels to hotels. Two of the best hostels are **Ashlee House** (3, E1 ☎ 7833 9400; www.ashleehouse.co.uk; 261-265 Gray's Inn Rd WC1 ⊖ King's Cross St Pancras) and the **Generator** (3, D2 ☎ 7388 7655; www.the-generator.co.uk; Compton Place, 37 Tavistock Place WC1 ⊖ Russell Sq). There are no age restrictions and singles/doubles (from £36/48) are available, as is dormitory accommodation (£12.50 to £19).

About London

HISTORY

Today's diverse, exciting metropolis had its genesis in the Roman city of Londinium, established on the Thames River in AD 43. For the full story on how one developed into the other over the centuries, visit the Museum of London (see p31).

The Celts & Romans

While the Celts settled on the Thames' southern bank, the Romans are generally credited as London's founders, as they turned the area north of the river into an impressive walled settlement in the 1st century AD. They built a bridge and made the city an important port and trade hub.

The Saxons & Danes

As the Roman empire crumbled, Londinium was abandoned in AD 410. The Saxons (northern Teutonic tribes) then moved into the area immediately to the west. The increasingly successful Saxon city came under sustained attack from the Danes (or Vikings) between 842 and the early 11th century. The Danish leader Canute was briefly king of England from 1016 to 1040. After Canute's death, the Saxon king Edward the Confessor moved his court to Westminster and founded an abbey nearby.

The Normans

Edward the Confessor's subsequent death created a power vacuum, which was filled by a Norman invasion from northern France. After his victory at the Battle of Hastings in 1066, William the Conqueror controlled the largest, richest and most powerful city in the Saxon kingdom. While the Norman ruler distrusted the 'vast and fierce populace' of London and raised the White Tower, the core of the Tower of London, he also confirmed the city's right to self-government.

Tudor London

Medieval London continued to prosper, but under the Tudors it really created a stir. Henry VIII's desire to divorce the first of his eight wives led him to break with the Catholic church and establish the Church of England

A dome not to be outdone: even WWII bombing couldn't blow St Paul's impressive top

in 1534. Henry's powerful daughter Elizabeth I (r 1558–1603) died without an heir, and the questions over succession combined with the weak rule of her Catholic relatives James I and Charles I to weaken the monarchy's grip on the country. During the English Civil War (1642–46), Oliver Cromwell's Roundheads (a coalition of Puritans, Parliamentarians and merchants) wrested complete control of the country from the king in 1646. However, Parliament restored the monarchy in 1660. London suffered a major setback soon afterwards, when the Great Fire of 1666 razed medieval, Tudor and Jacobean buildings to the ground. But the inferno wasn't

> **Wren's Churches**
> The greatest architect thus far to leave his mark on London was the influential Sir Christopher Wren (1632–1723). After the Great Fire of 1666 destroyed 88 of the city's churches, Wren was commissioned to rebuild 51 of them, as well as to create today's St Paul's Cathedral (see p19).
>
> Some 19 of the final 54 churches Wren went on to build have since been destroyed. However, many of his graceful Renaissance steeples still dot the skyline. Visit www.london -city-churches.org.uk for details.

without its silver linings: it wiped away the last vestiges of the plague of 1665, which killed 100,000, and it gave Christopher Wren a clean slate upon which to build (see the boxed text above).

Georgian Period

By 1700 there were 600,000 Londoners and, as the seat of Parliament and focus for a growing empire, the city was becoming ever richer and more important. Georgian architects such as John Nash, the planner of Trafalgar Square, and Sir John Soane (see Sir John Soane's Museum, p31) erected imposing symmetrical buildings and residential squares.

Victorian Age

The population exploded in the 19th century, creating vast suburbs to the south and east during Queen Victoria's 64-year reign and the Industrial Revolution. The number of inhabitants jumped from just under one million in 1800 to 6.5 million a century later.

WWII & the Post-War Period

Much of east London was obliterated during the Blitz of 1940–41, and by the time the war ended in 1945, 32,000 Londoners had been killed and another 50,000 seriously wounded. After the war, ugly housing and low-cost developments were hastily erected. The Thames docks, once an important economic mainstay, never recovered; shipping moved east to Tilbury, and the Docklands declined until redevelopment in the 1980s.

The post-war welfare state established by Labour was largely dismantled during 18 years of era-defining Conservative rule from 1979. Privatisation and deregulation were the mantras of the Thatcher years, leading to a boom in the financial services sector. However, political sleaze and voter disenchantment eventually helped shoo-in a Labour government under Prime Minister Tony Blair in 1997.

London Today

Initially, Blair's charisma, coupled with a strong economy, won over the capital's citizens, who contributed to Labour's second landslide in June

London by Numbers

- Central London population: 7.4 million
- Greater London population: 12.8 million
- Central London GDP per head: £19,500
- London's share of UK GDP: 16.5%
- Average house price: £210,100
- Annual overseas visitors: 11.6 million
- Average visitor expenditure per day: £77
- Inflation (Consumer Price Index): 1.3%
- Unemployment: 6.9%

2001. But subsequent unpopular decisions by the PM, including UK involvement in the 2003 Iraq war, saw Londoners increasingly unite behind their mayor, Ken Livingstone, instead.

ENVIRONMENT

Recent research by King's College, University of London, has found that breathing London's air is as bad as smoking 15 cigarettes a day. The study was conducted just after the introduction of mayor Ken Livingstone's 'congestion charge', which levies £5 a day against car owners who bring their vehicles into central London from 7am to 6.30pm on a weekday and has since reduced traffic by 10% to 15%. However, those with respiratory problems should still heed air-quality forecasts in weather bulletins, especially in summer.

Further plans are afoot to clean up the capital's air and its streets, where 177,000 tonnes of litter are dropped each year. Despite its murky appearance, the River Thames has undergone decontamination since the 1970s and is home to scores of fish and bird species.

GOVERNMENT & POLITICS

London has improved markedly since regaining control of its own affairs in the 21st century. After 1986, when Prime Minister Margaret Thatcher abolished the Greater London Council (GLC), the city spent 14 years as the only world capital without a self-governing authority or mayor. That finally changed when Tony Blair's Labour government established a new Greater London Authority (GLA) and the public elected former GLC leader Ken Livingstone as mayor in May 2000. The GLA has strategic influence over transport, economic development, environmental policy, police, fire brigades, civil defence and culture.

The congestion charge (see Environment earlier), Livingstone's flagship policy as mayor, has helped make his reign a success. So, having expelled the left-winger for running independently against its official mayoral candidate in 2000, the Labour Party threw its weight behind him for the 2004 election. Livingstone has also won Londoners' confidence with his efforts to improve the

The distinctive, spherical City Hall

Underground, housing and the environment. Mayoral elections were looming as we were going to press. Incumbent Ken Livingstone was the favourite, but by the time you read this the city just might have a new leader.

The governance of the City of London financial district is an administrative rather than electoral matter. The City is run by the Corporation of London, headed by the lord mayor.

ECONOMY

With a GDP of about £150 billion, London is Europe's richest city and the driving force behind the British economy. Indeed, the mayor's office estimates the capital subsidises the rest of the country to the tune of £9 to £15 billion a year in tax revenues.

Service industries are the biggest economic contributors. The financial and business services sector accounts for about 35% of turnover, followed by the creative and media sector. Tourism is another significant earner.

In recent years, the UK economy has consistently outperformed that of euro-zone countries. Unemployment and inflation remain relatively low and the capital is still experiencing a property boom. Although rich, London has a great disparity of wealth. While male professionals earn a third more in gross weekly earnings than the UK average, areas of London are among England's most deprived.

SOCIETY & CULTURE

Londoners are often as reserved and standoffish as reputed – commuters avert their eyes and travel in silence on the tube and trains. But London is extremely crowded and such behaviour is a way of coping with the constant crush of people.

On the plus side, Londoners are a tolerant bunch, unfazed by outrageous dress or behaviour. Indeed, they are whizzes at ignoring anyone trying to draw attention to themselves. In general, this means relatively low levels of chauvinism, sexism and racism.

This is also a very cosmopolitan city: 29% of Londoners hail from ethnic minority communities.

> **North–South Divide**
> Although the Thames isn't the physical barrier it was in the Middle Ages, psychologically the gulf is as wide as ever. Many people in north London refuse to believe there's anything of importance south of the river and jokes abound about needing a visa to cross.

Dos & Don'ts

It's not easy to cause offence in London. But try starting a general conversation at a bus stop or on a tube platform and you'll find people reacting as if you were mad; many Londoners would no more speak to a stranger in the street than fly to the moon. If you're obviously a tourist in need of directions, however, there won't be a problem.

DRESS

London is very relaxed about what you wear, but it pays to be respectful in places of worship. A few posh restaurants and many clubs operate dress codes. In the former, that usually means a jacket and tie for men, and no jeans or trainers for anyone; whether you gain admission to a club very much depends on whether you look cool and fashionable enough.

THE UNDERGROUND

The tube has its own etiquette. The most important rule is to stand on the right on escalators so that people can rush by on the left. Move along platforms, to prevent crowds blocking the entrance and, when a train arrives, stand aside until passengers have left the carriage. In some stations, you'll need to mind the gap between the train and the platform.

ARTS

London's wide-ranging cultural life is its greatest asset, whether you're talking classical paintings at the National Gallery or live music gigs.

Dance

The city that gave the world the all-male version of *Swan Lake* still produces the best in modern dance. Artists to watch out for include Matthew Bourne (the choreographer of that *Swan Lake*, *The Car Man*, *Nutcracker!* and *Play without Words*), Ballet Boyz' Michael Nunn and William Levitt, and south Asian dancers such as Akram Khan.

The new Laban centre has provided a shot in the arm to a very healthy scene, as has the recent refurbishment of the legendary Sadler's Wells theatre. Those who prefer classical ballet might enjoy Darcey Bussell, Sylvie Guillem or Irek Mukhamedov performing at the Royal Ballet. For further details on venues, see p90.

Film

London has never had an auteur to chronicle it in the same way that Woody Allen has New York. However, from 1950s Ealing comedies, such as *Passport to Pimlico*, *The Lavender Hill Mob* and *The Ladykillers*, to recent romantic comedies such as *Four Weddings and a Funeral*, *Bridget Jones's Diary* and *Love, Actually*, the city has provided a backdrop to many much-loved hits. Gangster flicks (eg Guy Ritchie's *Lock, Stock and Two Smoking Barrels*), gritty working-class dramas (Mike Leigh's *Secrets & Lies*) and popular fantasy (scenes from the Harry Potter films) have also been shot here.

Literature

Novelists of the calibre of Charles Dickens *(Oliver Twist)* have left a sterling legacy of London-oriented fiction, but that has never overawed modern writers such as Doris Lessing *(London Observed)*, Martin Amis *(London Fields, Money)*, Will Self *(Grey Area)* and Ian McEwan *(Atonement)*, to name just a few.

London writing ranges from the populist (Nick Hornby's *High Fidelity*) to the highbrow (Virginia Woolf's *Mrs Dalloway*), and has recently included a strong vein of fiction by writers from ethnic minority backgrounds, such as Hanif Kureishi's *The Buddha of Suburbia*, Zadie Smith's *White Teeth* and Monica Ali's *Brick Lane*.

Brick Lane – literary terrain

One of the best books about this extremely literate city is Peter Ackroyd's *London: The Biography* (2000), which weaves a fascinating tapestry of the capital's life and history.

Music

Despite a wealth of classical talent, London is best known for its popular music. It was the global epicentre of the swinging '60s, when the Beatles, Rolling Stones and Kinks ruled the airwaves. In the '70s, it launched punk rock on an unsuspecting world, in the '80s it produced new wave, and in the '90s Britpop bands such as Oasis, Pulp and Blur made an impact on global sales. In the noughties, New York seems to have snatched the baton as the world leader in popular music, as it does periodically. However, bands such as Coldplay and Radiohead still fly the flag for British music, rap artists such as Ms Dynamite continue to stimulate interest, and popular UK groups, from rockers the Darkness to music-press darlings Franz Ferdinand, all play London at regular intervals.

Of Rakes & Harlots

William Hogarth (1697–1764) was an artist and engraver who specialised in satire, and his moralising engravings offer an invaluable look at life among the lowly in Georgian London. His eight-plate series *A Harlot's Progress* traces the life of a country lass, from London ingénue to convicted whore. In *A Rake's Progress*, the debauched protagonist is seen being entertained in a Russell St tavern by a bevy of prostitutes.

Hogarth's works can be seen in Sir John Soane's Museum (p31), Tate Britain (p20) and the National Gallery (p14).

Painting

British painters have never dominated a particular epoch or style in the same way as their European counterparts. Arguably the only all-time great has been the early-19th-century romantic landscape painter JMW Turner. However, this is not to discount the works of Thomas Gainsborough, William Hogarth, John Constable, Francis Bacon or Lucian Freud.

The high-profile Britart movement of the 1990s launched conceptual artists such as Damien Hirst, Rachel Whiteread and Tracey Emin on the world. You can still see their work in the Saatchi Gallery (p28).

Theatre

From Shakespeare to the Angry Young Men of the 1960s, when the likes of John Osborne, Harold Pinter and Tom Stoppard stormed the London stage, the English capital has long been a dramatic colossus. Recent cross-fertilisation between the innovative fringe and the commercial West End means its theatre is the most exciting in the world right now. For more details on why, see pp89–90.

Vilar Floral Hall, Royal Opera House (p91)

Directory

A great way to avoid London's congestion charge

ARRIVAL & DEPARTURE

London can be reached by air from almost anywhere, and by bus, train and boat from Ireland and Continental Europe. There are direct connections from the USA, Australasia and European cities.

Air

London has five main airports: Heathrow, the largest, followed by Gatwick, Stansted, London City and Luton. Most major airlines have ticket offices in London; check 'Airlines' in the Yellow Pages (www.yell.co.uk) for details.

HEATHROW
Information

Approximately 15 miles (24km) west of central London, **Heathrow** (LHR; 1, B1 ☎ 0870 000 0123; www.baa.com/heathrow) is the world's busiest international airport; it has four terminals, with a fifth under construction and a sixth mooted. Each terminal has currency-exchange facilities, information counters and accommodation desks.

Most flights are through Terminals 1, 2 and 3. Airlines using Terminal 4 include Air Malta; British Airways (BA) for intercontinental flights excluding Miami; BA European flights to Amsterdam, Brussels, Copenhagen, Geneva, Lyon, Oslo, Paris, Vienna and Zurich; Emirates Abu Dhabi flights operated by BA; Kenya Airways; Qantas Airways; and Sri Lankan Airlines.

Airport Access

Train The fastest way into central London is on the **Heathrow Express** (☎ 0845 600 1515; www.heathrowexpress.co.uk; single/return £13/25, children free ☽ 15min, every 15min 5.10am-11.30pm) linking the airport with Paddington station (2, C3).

Underground The cheapest way to travel between Heathrow and central London is on London Underground's **Piccadilly line** (£3.80 ☽ 1hr, every 5-10min 5.30am-11.45pm). Of the two tube stations, one serves Terminals 1, 2 and 3, and the other serves Terminal 4. Each station has ticket machines and offices.

Bus Connecting King's Cross St Pancras with all Heathrow terminals, via Baker St tube station, Marble Arch and Notting Hill Gate, is **Airbus A2** (☎ 0870 574 7777; www.nationalexpress.com; single/return from £8/15 ☽ 1½hr, 5.30am-10pm from Heathrow; every 30min at peak times). The **Hotel Hoppa bus** (☎ 8400 6659; £3 ☽ every 15min 5.30am-9pm, then every 30min until 11.30pm) runs to 15 hotels near the airport.

Taxi A black cab to/from central London costs about £45 to £55.

GATWICK
Information

The smaller but better-organised **Gatwick** (LGW; 1, C2 ☎ 0870 000 2468; www.baa.com/gatwick) is 30 miles (48km) south of central London. The North and South Terminals are linked by a monorail service; journey time between the two is two minutes. Charters, scheduled airlines and no-frills carrier easyJet fly from Gatwick.

Airport Access

Train The handy **Gatwick Express** (☎ 0845 850 1530; www.gatwickexpress.co.uk; single/return £11/21.50 ☽ 30min; every 15min 5.50am-1.35am, plus earlier train at 5.20am) links the South Terminal station with Victoria station. **Connex South Central** (☎ 0845 748 4950; www.southcentraltrains.co.uk; £8 ☽ every 15-20min during peak times) runs slower but cheaper trains to/from Victoria station. **Thameslink** (☎ 0845 748 4950; www.thameslink.co.uk; from £10) has a service to/from King's Cross, Farringdon and London Bridge.

Bus Between 6am and 11pm **Airbus No 025** (☎ 0870 574 7777; www.nationalexpress.com; single/ return £5/10 ☾ 18 per day) operates from Victoria Coach Station to Gatwick (to London: 4.15am to 9.15pm).

Taxi A black cab to/from central London costs around £80 to £85.

STANSTED
Information
London's third-busiest international gateway, **Stansted** (STN ☎ 0870 000 0303; www.baa.com/ stansted) is 35 miles (56km) northeast of central London. Once relatively quiet, it's been turned into Europe's fastest-growing airport by the success of the no-frills carriers **Ryanair** (www.ryanair.com) and easyJet.

Airport Access
Train Take the **Stansted Express** (☎ 0845 748 4950; www.stansted express.com; single/return £13.80/ 24 ☾ 45min, every 15min 8am-5.30pm, otherwise every 30min) to go to Liverpool St station (3, DJ) 6am to midnight (to airport 5am to 11pm).

Bus Linking Stansted with Victoria Coach Station is **Airbus A6** (☎ 0870 574 7777; www.national express.com; single/return from £6/15 ☾ every 20min 5.30am-midnight). The sister A7 service operates overnight, every 15 minutes, via Liverpool St station.

Taxi A black cab to/from central London costs about £100 to £105.

LONDON CITY
Information
In the Docklands, 6 miles (10km) east of central London, **London City Airport** (LCY; 1, C1 ☎ 7646 0000; www.londoncityairport.com), is largely a business airport. It serves 22 Continental European and eight national destinations.

Airport Access
Bus The blue airport **Shuttlebus** (☎ 7646 0088; www.londoncity airport.com/shuttlebus) connects London City with Liverpool St station and Canary Wharf (£3.50/ 7 ☾ 10min; every 10min 6.50am-10pm). The green airport **Shuttlebus** (☎ 7646 0088; www.london cityairport.com/shuttlebus; single/ return £3/7 ☾ 10min, every 10min 6am-10.20pm) links London City and Canning Town tube, DLR and rail station.

Taxi A black cab to/from central London costs about £25 to £30.

LUTON
Information
A small airport roughly 35 miles (56km) north of central London, **Luton** (LTN ☎ 01582 405100; www.london-luton.co.uk) is the main base of low-cost airline **easyJet** (☎ 0870 600 0000; www .easyjet.com) and smaller charter flights.

Airport Access
Train Take **Thameslink** (☎ 0845 748 4950; www.thameslink.co.uk) for trains from King's Cross and other central London stations to Luton Airport Parkway station (£10.40; 30-40min, every 15min 7am-10pm), where there's a shuttle bus to the airport (eight minutes).

Bus Bus No 757 by **Green Line** (☎ 0870 608 7261; www.greenline .co.uk; single/return £8.50/12.50 ☾ 1¼hr, every 20min 8am-5pm, hourly 4am-8am & 5pm-2am) serves Luton, departing from Buckingham Palace Rd south of Victoria station.

Taxi A black cab to/from central London costs £95 to £100.

Bus
WITHIN THE UK
Bus travellers arrive at/depart from **Victoria Coach Station** (2, D5 ☎ 7730 3466; 164 Buckingham Palace Rd SW1). Queues can be long, so try to book by phone (☎ 7730 3499 ☺ 8.30am-7pm Mon-Fri, 8.30am-3.30pm Sat). **National Express** (☎ 0870 580 8080; www.nationalexpress.com) is the largest operator, and a Eurolines affiliate. There are smaller competitors on main UK routes, such as **Green Line** (☎ 0870 608 7261; www.greenline.co.uk).

CONTINENTAL EUROPE
It's still possible to get to/from Continental Europe by bus without using the Channel Tunnel. Book tickets direct through **Eurolines** (3, B6 ☎ 0870 514 3219; www.eurolines.com; 52 Grosvenor Gardens SW1) or through National Express, at Victoria Coach Station or via travel agents.

Train
WITHIN THE UK
The main national rail routes are served by InterCity trains, which can travel up to 140 miles/hr (225km/h). However, with the privatised service known for its inefficiency, don't be surprised if there are delays. Same-day returns and one-week advance purchase are the cheapest tickets for those without rail passes (which are available from mainline train stations). **National Rail Enquiries** (☎ 0845 748 4950; www.rail.co.uk) has timetables and fares.

CONTINENTAL EUROPE
For European train enquiries contact **Rail Europe** (☎ 0870 584 8848; www.raileurope.com).

Eurostar
Travelling via the Channel Tunnel, the high-speed passenger rail service **Eurostar** (☎ 0870 518 6186 or 01233-617575 from outside the UK; www.eurostar.com) links London's Waterloo station (3, E5) with Paris' Gare du Nord (three hours; up to 25 per day) and Brussels (two hours 40 minutes; up to 12 per day); some trains also stop at Lille and Calais in France. Fares vary enormously. To Paris or Brussels, for example, costs between £59 for a cheap APEX return (booked at least 21 days in advance, staying a Saturday night) and £300 for the maximum return fare.

Le Shuttle
Trains run by **Le Shuttle** (☎ 0870 535 3535; www.eurotunnel.com) transport motor vehicles and bicycles between Folkestone in England and Coquelles in France (near Calais). They run up to every 15 minutes (hourly 1am to 6am). Booking online is cheapest, where a two- to five-day excursion fare costs from £105, pre-purchased day returns from £40 and same-day returns from £100. All prices include a car and passengers.

Travel Documents
Passport
Passports must be valid for six months from date of entry.

Visa
Visas aren't required by nationals of Australia, Canada, New Zealand, South Africa and the USA for stays of up to six months; EU citizens don't require a visa and can stay indefinitely. Others should check www.ukvisas.gov.uk.

Visa regulations may change, so check with your local British embassy, high commission or consulate before leaving home.

Return/Onward Ticket

A return ticket may be required and you may need to prove that you have sufficient funds to support yourself; a credit card will help.

Customs & Duty-Free

Like all EU nations, the UK has a two-tier customs system: one for goods bought duty-free and one for goods bought in an EU country where taxes and duties have already been paid.

The limits for goods purchased duty-free outside the EU are 200 cigarettes or 250g of tobacco; 2L of still wine plus 1L of spirits over 22% or another 2L wine (sparkling or still); 50g of perfume, 250cc of toilet water; and other goods (including cider and beer) up to £145.

You can buy items in another EU country, where they might be cheaper, and bring them into the UK, provided duty and tax have been paid. Allowances are 800 cigarettes; 200 cigars and 1kg of tobacco; 10L of spirits; 20L of fortified wines; 90L of wine (sparkling limited to 60L); and 110L of beer.

Left Luggage

There are left-luggage facilities (£5 per item per day) at Heathrow's **Terminal 1** (☎ 8745 5301 ⏱ 6am-11pm), **Terminal 2** (☎ 8745 4599 ⏱ 5.30am-10.30pm), **Terminal 3** (☎ 8759 3344 ⏱ 5.30am-10.30pm) and **Terminal 4** (☎ 8745 7460 ⏱ 5am-11pm). All can forward baggage.

There are left-luggage offices at Gatwick at the **North Terminal** (☎ 01293-502013 ⏱ 6am-10pm) and **South Terminal** (☎ 01293-502014 ⏱ 24hr).

GETTING AROUND

Despite the decrepit state of the Underground, the tube is still the best way to traverse this enormous city, because it avoids road traffic. The new congestion charge (see Car & Motorcycle, p114) has meant buses run better, but they're still slower than the tube. Registered black cabs are expensive. For general information about the Underground, buses, Docklands Light Railway (DLR) or local trains call ☎ 7222 1234 or visit www.tfl.gov.uk. For news of how services are running, call **Travelcheck** (☎ 7222 1200).

Travel Passes

One-day Travelcards can be used after 9.30am weekdays (anytime on weekends) on all transport – the tube, main-line trains, the DLR and buses (including night buses). Most visitors find a one-day Travelcard for Zones 1 and 2 (£4.30/2 adult/concession) is sufficient. Before 9.30am Monday to Friday, you need a Peak Travelcard (£5.30/2.60) for Zones 1 and 2.

A weekly Travelcard for Zones 1 and 2, valid any time of day, costs £20.20/8.20. A weekend Travelcard valid Saturday and Sunday in Zones 1 and 2 costs £6.40/3. Family Travelcards are also available.

Underground

The Underground's 12 lines extend as far as Buckinghamshire, Essex and Heathrow. There are Underground travel information centres at all Heathrow terminals, a half-dozen major tube stations and at larger main-line train stations. Services run from 5.30am (7am on Sunday) to roughly midnight.

The Underground is divided into six concentric zones. The basic fare for Zone 1 is £2/60p for adults/children; to cross all six zones (eg, to/from Heathrow) costs £3.80/1.50. A carnet of 10 tickets for Zone 1 costs £15/5. If you're travelling through a couple of zones or several times in one day, consider a Travelcard (see p113).

Tickets can be bought from machines or counters at the entrance to each station.

Bus

Buses run regularly between 7am and midnight; less frequent night buses (prefixed with the letter *N*) take over between midnight and 7am.

Single-journey bus tickets (valid for two hours) cost £1/40p adult/child and day passes are £2.50/1 adult/child. In central London, at stops with yellow signs, you must buy your ticket *before* boarding, from the automatic machine. Otherwise, you can purchase your ticket on boarding the bus.

Trafalgar Square (6, E6), Tottenham Court Rd (6, C1), and Oxford Circus (6, A1), are the main termini for night buses.

The *Central London Bus Guide Map* and several individual area maps are free from most travel information centres.

DLR & Train

The driverless Docklands Light Railway links the City at Bank and Tower Gateway at Tower Hill, with services to Stratford to the east and the Docklands and Greenwich to the south. The DLR runs weekdays 5.30am to 12.30am (shorter hours at weekends); fares are as for the tube (see p113). For general information on the DLR call ☎ 7363 9700 or visit www.dlr.co.uk. For news of how the DLR and Docklands bus services are running, call the 24-hour Docklands Travel Hotline on ☎ 7918 4000.

Other passenger trains are operated by **Silverlink** (the North London line ☎ 0845 601 4867/8; www.silverlink-trains.com), which links Richmond in the southwest with North Woolwich in the south-

east; and **Thameslink** (☎ 0845 748 4950; www.thameslink.co.uk), running from London Bridge through the City to King's Cross and Luton. Most lines interchange with the tube, and Travelcards can be used on both systems.

Taxi

Drivers of licensed black cabs have undergone extensive training to obtain 'the knowledge' of every central London street, so you're sure to arrive at your destination. Cabs are available for hire when the yellow light above the windscreen is lit. Fares are metered, with flag fall at £1.60 and each successive kilometre costing 90p. To order a black cab by phone, try **Dial-a-Cab** (☎ 7253 5000); you must pay by credit card and will be charged a 15% premium.

Minicabs, some of which are now licensed, are cheaper competitors to cabs. However, they can only be hired by phone or from a minicab office; every neighbourhood and high street has one. Some minicab drivers also have a limited idea of how to get around efficiently – or safely. Minicabs can carry up to four people and don't have meters, so get a quote before you start. Bargaining is sometimes acceptable.

Small companies are based in particular areas. Try a large 24-hour operator: ☎ 7387 8888, 7272 2222/3322 or 8888 4444.

Car & Motorcycle

If you bring your car into central London from 7am to 6.30pm on a weekday, you'll need to pay a £5 per day congestion charge (motorbikes are exempt). The current charge zone is roughly south of Euston Rd, west of Commercial St (near Liverpool St station), north of Kennington Lane and east of Park Lane. However, plans are afoot to extend this.

There's a large letter *C* in a red circle at the start of the zone. Having passed this, you must pay the £5 charge before 10pm on the same day, or £10 between 10pm and midnight, to avoid receiving an £80 fine. Traffic cameras note vehicle licence plates and the authorities have links to international agencies, so even European visitors driving their own car must pay. If hiring a vehicle, check arrangements with your hire company.

You can pay the charge by phone on ☎ 0845 900 1234 or at newsagents, petrol stations and any shop displaying the *C* sign. Alternatively, you can register online at www.cclondon.com and then pay by mobile phone text message. Further details are on the website.

Parking in central London is difficult to find. Traffic wardens and wheel clampers are extremely efficient and if your vehicle is towed away, it will cost at least £125 to get it back. If your car is clamped, ring ☎ 7747 4747 (24 hours) to get it back.

Road Rules

Vehicles travel on the left side of the road; give way to your right at roundabouts. Wearing a seat belt is always compulsory in the front seat and in the back when fitted. Motorcyclists must wear helmets. Speed limits are 30mph (48km/h) in built-up areas, 60mph (96km/h) on single carriageways, and 70mph (112km/h) on motorways and dual carriageways. A blood-alcohol level of 0.08% (80mg/100mL per litre of blood) is the limit while driving. You can get a copy of the *Highway Code* from AA or RAC outlets.

Rental

Hiring cars from as little as £15 per day, **EasyCar** (☎ 0906 333 3333; www.easycar.com) is the capital's cheapest rental firm. (The company has refuted a major newspaper story about shoddy service.) Otherwise, major rental firms, such as **Budget** (☎ 0870 156 5656; www.budget.co.uk) and **Hertz** (☎ 0870 599 6699; www .hertz.com), charge from £45 a day and £150 to £200 a week for their smallest cars.

Driving Licence & Permits

Your normal driving licence is legal for 12 months after you enter the UK. Otherwise, an International Driving Permit (IDP), is obtainable from your local motoring association for a fee.

PRACTICALITIES
Climate & When to Go

London is a year-round destination. High season is June to August, with a better chance of good weather but also crowds and sold-out venues. In April/May or September/October the weather can still be good, and queues are shorter. November to March are quieter. Expect cool weather and rain even in high summer.

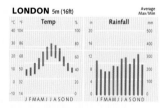

LONDON 5m (16ft)

Disabled Travellers

London isn't the easiest city for travellers with impaired movement. Access to the Underground is pretty limited, while uneven pavements and crowding make life difficult for wheelchair users. Newer buses sometimes have steps that lower for easier access, and there are two dedicated bus services offering disabled access: Nos 205 and 705. The more useful 205 runs from Paddington to Whitechapel. The 705 runs from Victoria to Waterloo and London Bridge. Both operate from 6am to midnight.

For further information check with **Transport for London's Access & Mobility** (☎ 7222 1234 or textphone 7918 3015; Windsor House, 42/50 Victoria St, London SW1 9TN).

Information & Organisations
The **Royal Association for Disability and Rehabilitation** (RADAR ☎ 7250 3222; www.radar.org.uk; Unit 12, City Forum, 250 City Rd, London EC1V 8AF) is an umbrella organisation of disability groups and a useful source of information.

Discounts
Most attractions offer discounts to children (check each venue for age limits), youth card–holders under 25 (or 26), students with ISIC cards (age limits may apply), those over 60 (or 65; sometimes lower for women), disabled visitors and families.

The **London Pass** (☎ 0870 242 9988; www.londonpass.com) allows free admission to over 70 museums and other attractions (see individual listings for details), and unlimited travel on the tube (Zones 1-6), buses and trains within central London. The pass costs £32/55/71/110 for 1/2/3/6 days (£20/34/45/61 for those aged five to 15).

Student, Youth & Teachers' Cards
The International Student Identity Card (ISIC), the International Youth Travel Card (IYTC) issued by the Federation of International Youth Travel Organisations (FIYTO) and the International Teacher Identity Card (ITIC) can produce discounts on many forms of transport and admission to venues.

Seniors' Cards
Many attractions offer reduced price admission for those aged over 60 or 65 (sometimes as low as 55 for women); ask if you can't see a discount listed. The railways offer a Senior Rail Card (£18) for those aged over 60.

Electricity
The standard voltage throughout Britain is 230/240V AC, 50Hz. Plugs have three square pins, but adapters for European-style plugs are widely available.

Embassies & High Commissions
Australian High Commission (6, E2 ☎ 7379 4334; www.australia.org.uk; Australia House, Strand WC2 ✆ Temple/Holborn)

Canadian High Commission (3, D4 ☎ 7258 6600; www.canada.org.uk; Canada House, 5 Trafalgar Sq SW1 ✆ Charing Cross) For visas, go to 38 Grosvenor St W1 (3, B4 ✆ Bond St).

French Consulate-General (2, C5 ☎ 09065 540700, 7073 1250; www.ambafrance.org.uk; 21 Cromwell Rd SW7 ✆ South Kensington)

New Zealand High Commission (3, D4 ☎ 7930 8422; www.nzembassy.com; New Zealand House, 80 Haymarket SW1 ✆ Piccadilly Circus)

South African High Commission (6, D4 ☎ 7451 7299; www.southafricahouse.com; South Africa House, Trafalgar Sq WC2 ✆ Charing Cross)

US Embassy (3, A4 ☎ 09068 200290, 7499 9000; www.usembassy.org.uk; 5 Upper Grosvenor St W1 ✆ Bond St)

Emergencies

London is remarkably safe considering its size and uneven wealth. Generally, be careful at night and in crowded places such as the tube, where pickpockets and bag snatchers operate.

Ambulance, Fire & Police ☎ 999

Fitness

Gyms

The conveniently located **Oasis Sports Centre** (6, D1 ☎ 7831 1804; 32 Endell St WC2 ⊕ Covent Garden) has heated indoor and outdoor 25m pools, gymnasium facilities as well as squash and badminton courts. A dip will cost you £3. Ring for court hire and gym use.

Horse Riding

Hire horses at **Hyde Park Stables** (2, C4 ☎ 7723 2813; www.hyde parkstables.com; 63 Bathurst Mews W2 ⊕ Lancaster Gate). Prices are £40 to £60 hourly, depending on the day and the rider's experience.

Pools, Spas & Baths

Two traditional spas include the **Art Deco Porchester Spa** (2, C3 ☎ 7792 3980; Porchester Centre, Queensway W2; adult/couple £18.95/£26.75 ⊕ Bayswater/Royal Oak) and **Ironmonger Row Baths** (3, G1 ☎ 7253 4011; Ironmonger Row EC1; turkish bath £6.50-11; swim £3.10 ⊕ Old St). Both offer mixed and separate sessions for men and women; call for details.

You can go outdoor swimming at the mixed, men's and women's ponds on **Hampstead Heath** (☎ 7485 4491 🕓 7am-dusk 🚉 Hampstead Heath/Gospel Oak), although the men's pond is very much a gay cruising ground. There are many other swimming pools across the city, including lidos (outdoor pools); check 'swimming pools' or 'leisure centres' in the Yellow Pages (www.yell.co.uk).

Tennis

The **Lawn Tennis Association** (☎ 7381 7000; www.lta.org.uk; Queen's Club, Palliser Rd W14) produces pamphlets on where to play tennis in London; send a stamped addressed envelope.

Alternatively, check www.london tennis.co.uk for where to play; most London parks have courts.

Gay & Lesbian Travellers

Britain is fairly open-minded about homosexuality and London has a flourishing gay scene. But there remain pockets of out-and-out hostility, and overt displays of affection are not necessarily wise away from acknowledged gay venues and areas such as Old Compton St in Soho. The age of consent, as for heterosexuals, is 16.

Information & Organisations

There's a 24hr **Lesbian & Gay Switchboard** (☎ 7837 7324). For listings magazines, see p94.

Health

Immunisations

No jabs are needed to visit Britain.

Precautions

Tap water is safe. Food scares about British beef (bovine spongiform encephalopathy, BSE or 'mad-cow disease') and lamb (following the 2002 foot-and-mouth epidemic) are a distant memory.

Insurance & Medical Treatment

Reciprocal arrangements with the UK allow Australian residents and New Zealanders, among others, to obtain free emergency medical treatment through the National Health Service (NHS). However, travel insurance is still advisable to cover other major expenses, such as ambulance and repatriation.

Medical Services

EU nationals (with an E111 form) can get free emergency treatment. In mid-2004 a European Health Insurance Card was introduced that will eventually replace the E111 and other health forms.

Hospitals with 24-hour emergency units include:

Guy's Hospital (3, H5 ☎ 7955 5000; St Thomas St SE1 ⊖ London Bridge)

Royal Free Hospital (2, D1 ☎ 7794 0500; Pond St NW3 ⊖ Belsize Park)

University College Hospital (3, C2 ☎ 7387 9300; Grafton Way WC1 ⊖ Euston Square)

Dental Services

If you chip a tooth or require emergency treatment, head to **Eastman Dental Hospital** (3, E1 ☎ 7915 1000; 256 Gray's Inn Rd WC1 ⊖ King's Cross St Pancras).

Pharmacies

There's always a local chemist that opens 24 hours (see local papers). **Boots** (6, C3 ☎ 7734 6126; www.boots.com; 44-46 Regent St W1 ⊕ 9am-8pm ⊖ Piccadilly Circus) opposite the Eros statue opens late. So does **Pharmacentre** (2, D3 ☎ 7723 2336, 0808 108 7521; 149 Edgware Rd ⊕ 9am-midnight ⊖ Edgware Rd).

Holidays

New Year's Day	1 Jan
Good Friday	late Mar/Apr
Easter Monday	late Mar/Apr
May Day Bank Holiday	May (1st Mon)
Spring Bank Holiday	May (last Mon)
Summer Bank Holiday	Aug (last Mon)
Christmas Day	25 Dec
Boxing Day	26 Dec

Imperial System

The UK has legally switched to the metric system, but imperial equivalents are still frequently used. Distances continue to be given in miles, yards, feet and inches, although most liquids (apart from milk and beer, which come in half-pints and pints) are sold in litres. See the conversion table below.

TEMPERATURE

$°C = (°F - 32) ÷ 1.8$
$°F = (°C \times 1.8) + 32$

DISTANCE

1in = 2.54cm
1cm = 0.39in
1m = 3.3ft = 1.1yd
1ft = 0.3m
1km = 0.62 miles
1 mile = 1.6km

WEIGHT

1kg = 2.2lb
1lb = 0.45kg
1g = 0.04oz
1oz = 28g

VOLUME

1L = 0.26 US gallons
1 US gallon = 3.8L
1L = 0.22 imperial gallons
1 imperial gallon = 4.55L

Internet

London is chock-a-block with cybercafés. The largest chain is easyEverything, which has 15 outlets apart from those listed here (for details see their website: www.easyeverything.com).

Internet Cafés

BTR (3, C2 ☎ 7681 4223; www.be-the-reds.com; 39 Whitfield St W1; per 5min 50p ⊕ 9am-8pm Mon-Fri, 11am-7pm Sat & Sun ⊖ Goodge St). You can plug in your laptop here.

easyEverything (3, B6 ☎ 7233 8456; www.easyeverything.com; 9-13 Wilton Rd S W1 ⊕ 8am-midnight Tue-Sat, 8am-11pm Sun-Mon ⊖ Victoria) There is also a branch at 9–16 Tottenham Court Rd (3, C3 ⊕ 8am-midnight Sun-Wed, 8am-2am Thu-Sat ⊖ Tottenham Court Rd). It costs £1 for 10 minutes to one hour, depending on the time of day.

Useful Websites

The Lonely Planet website (www .lonelyplanet.com) offers a speedy link to many of London's websites. Others to try include:

BBC London (www.bbc.co.uk/London/ whereyoulive)

Evening Standard (www.thisislondon .co.uk)

Time Out (www.timeout.com)

UK Weather (www.met-office.gov.uk)

Lost Property

For items left on buses and tubes, visit Transport for **London's Lost Property Office** (3, A2; 200 Baker St NW1 5RZ ☽ 9.30am-2pm Mon-Fri ⊖ Baker St).

For items left on main-line trains, call ☎ 7928 5151, where you'll be redirected to the correct main terminal.

For items left in black cabs, call ☎ 7918 2000.

Money
Currency

The pound sterling (£) is divided into 100 pence (p). Coins of 1p and 2p are copper; 5p, 10p, 20p and 50p are silver; the heavy £1 coin is gold; and the £2 coin has a gold-coloured edge and silver centre. Notes (bills) come in £5, £10, £20 and £50 denominations. Britain is unlikely to adopt the euro anytime soon.

Travellers Cheques

Thomas Cook (☎ 01733-318950) and **American Express** (Amex ☎ 0870 600 1060) are widely accepted, don't charge for cashing their own cheques (though exchange rates are not always competitive) and can often replace lost or stolen cheques within 24 hours. Both have offices all over London.

Credit Cards

The following cards are widely accepted in London. For 24hr card cancellations or assistance, call:

Amex	☎ 01273-689955/ 696933
Diners Club	☎ 0800 460800, 01252-516261
JCB	☎ 7499 3000
MasterCard	☎ 0800 964767
Visa	☎ 0800 895082

ATMs

You'll find ATMs linked up to international money systems outside banks, at train stations and inside some pubs and retail outlets.

Changing Money

Changing money is easy in London, with banks, *bureaux de change* and travel agencies all competing for business. There are 24-hour exchange bureaus at Heathrow Terminals 1, 3 and 4 (Terminal 2 bureau opens 6am to 11pm).

The main offices for **Amex** (6, C3 ☎ 7484 9600; 30-31 Haymarket ☽ 9am-6pm Mon-Sat, 10am-5pm Sun ⊖ Piccadilly Circus), and **Thomas Cook** (3, C4 ☎ 7853 6400; 30 St James's St ☽ 9am-5.30pm Mon-Fri, from 10am Wed, 10am-4pm Sat ⊖ Green Park) are both centrally located.

London banks are usually open 9.30am to 5.30pm Monday to Friday, with some open 9.30am to noon on Saturday.

Newspapers & Magazines

Most major newspapers in the UK are national. The only true London papers are the paid-for afternoon tabloid, the *Evening Standard* and the morning freebie *Metro*.

The line between serious broadsheet newspapers and celebrity-obsessed tabloids has blurred in recent years. Indeed the formerly struggling *Independent* scored a huge success with its (highbrow) tabloid edition – a move that the centre-right *Times* promptly followed. With the traditionally best-selling broadsheet the *Telegraph* (a Conservative bastion) suffering, England's best-selling papers continued to be older tabloids such as the *Sun* and *Daily Mirror.*

The broadsheet *Guardian* is London's truly liberal paper; the middle-level tabloids, especially the *Daily Mail,* are more right-wing. See p78 for listings magazines.

Opening Hours

Offices   9/10am-5/5.30/6pm Mon-Fri
Shops   9/10am-6pm Mon-Sat (some
          10am-4pm or noon-6pm Sun)
Late-Night Shopping
          9/10am-8pm Thu in the West End

Photography & Video

Slide and print film are widely available. Try **Jessops** (6, D1 ☎ 7240 6077; 63-69 New Oxford St WC1 ⊖ Tottenham Court Rd), which has branches throughout the city, or any branch of Boots (see Pharmacies, p118).

The UK, like most of Europe and Australia, uses the PAL video system, which is incompatible with the American and Japanese NTSC system.

Post

The Royal Mail, Britain's postal service, offers a two-class service, with letters bearing a 1st-class stamp delivered in a day or two and those with a 2nd-class stamp within a week. You can buy stamps at post-office counters, vending machines outside post offices and at selected newsagents and corner shops.

For general postal enquiries call ☎ 0845 722 3344 or visit www.royalmail.com.

London post offices usually open Monday to Friday 8.30am or 9am to 5pm or 5.30pm, with some main ones open Saturday 9am to noon or 1pm. The Trafalgar Square post office (GPO/poste restante; on William IV St) opens Monday to Friday 8.30am to 6.30pm and Saturday 9am to 5.30pm.

Postal Rates

Domestic 1st-/2nd-class mail (up to 60g) costs 20/28p; postcards to Europe/Australasia and the Americas cost 38/42p.

Radio

London radio stations include pop station Capital FM (95.8FM) and Capital Gold (1548AM), which plays '60s–'80s oldies. BBC London Live (94.9FM) is a talk-back station. Xfm (104.9FM) is an alternative radio station playing indie music.

Among the national stations are:

BBC Radio 1 (98.8FM) Pop/rock/dance.
BBC Radio 2 (89.1FM) '60s, '70s and '80s golden oldies.
BBC Radio 3 (91.3FM) Classical music and plays.
BBC Radio 4 (93.5FM) News, drama, talk.
Radio 5 Live (909AM) Sport and news.
BBC World Service (648AM) Coverage from around the world.
Jazz FM (102.2FM) Jazz and blues.
Classic FM (100.9FM) Classical music with commercials.

Telephone

Public phones, which are ubiquitous in London, are either coin-operated (minimum 20p) or accept phonecards or credit cards.

Phonecards

Local and international phonecards are available at newsagents, including British Telecom (BT) phonecards, which come in £3, £5, £10 and £20 denominations. Lonely Planet's ekit phonecard, specifically aimed at travellers, provides competitive international calls (avoid using it for local calls), messaging services and free email. Visit www.lonelyplanet.com/travel _services for details on joining and accessing the service.

Mobile Phones

The UK uses the GSM 900 network, which covers Continental Europe, Australia and New Zealand, but is incompatible with the North American GSM 1900 or Japan's system (some North Americans have GSM 1900/900 phones that do work here). You can rent a mobile from various companies, including **Mobell** (☎ 0800 243524; www.mobell.com) from £2.50 to £5 per day, plus £250 to £300 deposit.

Country & City Codes

UK	☎ 44
London	☎ (0) 20

Useful Numbers

Directory enquiries	☎ 118 118
International dialling code	☎ 00
International directory	☎ 153
Local & national operator	☎ 100
Reverse-charge/collect calls	☎ 155
Time	☎ 123
Weathercall	☎ 0906 850 0401

International Codes

Australia	☎ 0061
Canada	☎ 001
Japan	☎ 0081
New Zealand	☎ 0064
South Africa	☎ 0027
USA	☎ 001

TV

There are scores of satellite (including Sky TV), cable and digital channels available to subscribers. The five free-to-air channels, including two BBC channels with no commercials, are:

BBC1 *Fame Academy, Walking with Dinosaurs, Eastenders, BBC News.*

BBC2 *Weakest Link, University Challenge, Newsnight.*

ITV *Pop Idol, Who Wants to be a Millionaire, Stars in their Eyes, Blind Date, Coronation St, The Bill.*

Channel 4 *Friends, ER, Will & Grace, Channel 4 News, Channel 4 News, Hollyoaks, Countdown.*

Channel 5 Mainly reruns of '80s B-movies.

Time

The time in London, Greenwich Mean Time (GMT), is the world-wide standard against which other time is set. At noon GMT, it's:

7am in New York
4am in Los Angeles
1pm in Paris
2pm in Johannesburg
11pm in Sydney

From late March to late October, even London puts its clocks one hour ahead of GMT, for British Summer Time.

Tipping

Restaurants	10% to 15% (usually included)
Taxis	round up to nearest £
Porters	£2 per bag

Toilets

Public toilets in London are few and far between. Those at main train stations (20p) bus terminals and attractions are OK and sometimes have facilities for disabled people and those with young children.

Tourist Information

The Britain Visitor Centre run by the British Tourism Authority (BTA) and information centres run by Visit London, London's official tourist authority, handle walk-ins only. Otherwise, call the **BTA** (☎ 8846 9000; www.visit britain.com) or **Visit London** (☎ 7932 2000; www.visitlondon .com). Visit London has a **London Line** (☎ 09068 663344; per min 60p), with details on attractions, accommodation, tours, theatre, children's London and more.

Britain Visitor Centre

The **Britain and London Visitor Centre** (6, C4; 1 Regent St SW1 🕒 9.30am-6.30pm Mon, 9am-6.30pm Tue-Fri, 10am-4pm Sat & Sun ✛ Piccadilly Circus) offers tourist information; hotel, travel and theatre bookings; maps; and books. From June to September it's open 9am to 5pm on Saturday.

Tourist Information Centres

Visit Britain has a TIC at the Arrivals Hall in Waterloo's International Terminal (3, E5 ☎ 7928 6221 🕒 8.30am-10.30pm Mon-Sat, 9.30am-10.30pm Sun) and one at Greenwich (5, B2 ☎ 0870 608 2000; Pepys House, 2 Cutty Sark Gardens SE10 🕒 10am-5pm Mon-Sat, plus 10am-5pm Sun Jun-Sep).

You can also go to a Corporation of London **TIC** (3, G3 ☎ 7332 1456; St Paul's Churchyard EC4 🕒 9.30am-5pm Apr-Sep, 9.30am-5pm Mon-Fri, 9.30am-12.30pm Sat Oct-Mar ✛ St Paul's).

Women Travellers

Aside from the rare wolf whistle and unwelcome body contact on the tube, women will find male Londoners reasonably harmless. If you're over 16, you can buy the morning-after pill over the counter in many pharmacies.

Information & Organisations

Marie Stopes International (3, C2 ☎ 0845 300 8090; 108 Whitfield St W1 🕒 7am-10pm ✛ Warren St) provides contraception, sexual health checks and abortions. The **Rape & Sexual Abuse Helpline** (☎ 8683 3300) operates noon to 2.30pm and 7pm to 9.30pm Monday to Friday and 2.30pm to 5pm on weekends.

LANGUAGE

Although English is the official language, more than 300 languages are now spoken throughout the UK capital.

The variety of English spoken in London and the surrounding region is referred to as estuary English and is characterised by a glottal *t* (so that the word 'alright' sounds like 'orwhy'), a rising inflection and, in more recent years, a constant use of 'innit'.

For more insights, see Lonely Planet's *British Phrasebook*.

Standing guard at the Natural History Museum

Index

EATING

SLEEPING

SHOPPING

Sights Index

FEATURES

Sausage & Mash Cafe	*Eating*
Royal Albert Hall	*Entertainment*
Crown & Goose	*Drinking*
Big Ben	*Highlights*
Harrods	*Shopping*
London Dungeon	*Sights/Activities*
Metropolitan Hotel	*Sleeping*

AREAS

	Building
	Land
	Mall
	Other Area
	Park/Cemetary
	Sports
	Urban

HYDROGRAPHY

	River, Creek
	Intermittent River
	Canal
	Water

BOUNDARIES

	State, Provincial
	Regional, Suburb
	Ancient Wall

ROUTES

	Tollway
	Freeway
	Primary Road
	Secondary Road
	Tertiary Road
	Lane
	Under Construction
	One-Way Street
	Unsealed Road
	Mall/Steps
	Tunnel
	Walking Path
	Walking Trail
	Track
	Walking Tour

TRANSPORT

	Airport, Airfield
	Bus Route
	Ferry
	General Transport
	Underground Station
	Rail

SYMBOLS

	Bank, ATM
	Castle, Fortress
	Christian
	Embassy, Consulate
	Hospital, Clinic
	Information
	Internet Access
	Islamic
	Jewish
	Monument
	Point of Interest
	Police Station
	Post Office
	Swimming Pool
	Telephone
	Toilets
	Zoo, Bird Sanctuary

24/7 travel advice
www.lonelyplanet.com